PRAYER FOR PARISH GROUPS

D0067316

Donal Harrington & Julie Kavanagh

Prayer for Parish Groups

PREPARING AND LEADING PRAYER
FOR GROUP MEETINGS

Saint Mary's Press
Christian Brothers Publications
Winona, Minnesota

First published in 1998 by
Saint Mary's Press
Christian Brothers Publications
702 Terrace Heights
Winona, Minnesota 55987-1320
ISBN 0-88489-620-X

In association with The Columba Press, Dublin, Ireland

Cover by Bill Bolger
Origination by The Columba Press
Printed in Ireland by Colour Books Ltd, Dublin

Acknowledgements

The author and publisher gratefully acknowledge the permission of the following to quote from works within their copyright: Text by Brother Roger of Taizé © Ateliers et Presses de Taizé, 71250 Taizé Community, France; Ave Maria Press, Notre Dame, IN 46556 for *May I Have This Dance* (1992) and *Praying Our Goodbyes* (1988) by Joyce Rupp; Darton, Longman and Todd for *The Road to Daybreak* by Henri Nouwen (1989, 1997), *The Longest Journey* by John Dalyrymple (1979) and *Celtic Fire* by Robert Van de Weyer (1990); The Dedalus Press for *The Absent Fountain* by Paul Murray; Dominican Publications for *Windows on the Gospel* by Flor McCarthy; Farrar, Straus & Giroux for *Thoughts in Solitude* by Thomas Merton; Forest of Peace Publishing Inc., for *Prayers for the Servants of God* (1980) and *Prayers for a Planetary Pilgrim* (1989) by Edward Hays; Gujarat Sahitya Prakash, India for *Sadhana* and *The Song of the Bird* by Anthony de Mello; HarperCollins Publishers for *Seasons of Your Heart: Prayers and Reflections* by Macrina Wiederkehr; Dimension Books, Denville, NJ, for *Celtic Meditations* by Edward Farrell; Orbis Books and Lutterworth Press for *Revolutionary Patience* by Dorothee Sölle; Routledge for *A Celtic Miscellany: Translations from Celtic Literature* by Kenneth Hurlstone Jackson; SPCK, London for *Tides and Seasons* by David Adam (1989); SPCK, London and Morehouse Publishing, Harrisburg, PA, for *The Edge of Glory* by David Adam (1985); St Mary's Press, Winona MN for *Canticles and Gathering Prayers* by John P. Mossi and Suzanne Toolan (1989); St Paul's, London for *Through the Year With Words of Encouragement* by Daniel Cronin; Source Books, Trabuco Canyon, California for *I Hear A Seed Growing* and *There Was No Path So I Trod One* by Edwina Gateley; Twenty-Third Publications, Mystic, CT, for *Storytelling the Word* by William Bausch and *Prayer Services for Parish Meetings* by Debra Hintz.
We have made every effort to trace copyright and to seek permission to use quotations. If any involuntary infringement of copyright has occurred, we offer our apologies and will correct the omission in future editions.

Contents

Prayer Sessions for Various Times and Seasons

Preface

This is a book of prayer resources for parish groups. It is not a book for prayer groups, but a book for every parish group. For prayer is the heart of the work of any group engaged in parish ministry or parish renewal.

Often, however, prayer is not put at the heart of the work. Often there is no more than a cursory prayer at the start and end of the meeting – a bit like the referee's whistle starting and ending a football match. And even when the group tries to do something more substantial, many group members feel a lack of confidence and competence, not to mention a lack of texts and resources.

Prayer for Parish Groups is intended to address this situation. There are one hundred and eight different texts for group prayer, on a wide variety of themes. By 'text' we mean a two-page spread (for ease of photocopying) containing prayers, readings and reflections for a ten- to fifteen-minute time of prayer. So, if you are the one preparing the prayer for the next meeting, you need look no further. The alphabetical index at the end of the book will help you in choosing a suitable theme.

But there is more. The group's prayer isn't just a litany of words. It is an experience of the divine presence. Merely having a text is no guarantee that the prayer is going to be a moment of spiritual nourishment. With the text in hand, somebody has to *prepare* the time of prayer. Somebody has to think about setting the mood ... lighting a candle ... having music or not ... who will read what ... when to pause for silent prayer ... whether to have spontaneous shared prayer ... These are the kind of elements that turn a *prayer text* into a *prayer experience*.

And that is why the book begins with two short chapters – to help the person preparing the prayer to *work with the text.* The first chapter clarifies why prayer is so important for parish groups. If your group wants to make more of prayer, you might begin by discussing this chapter together. The second chapter is a step-by-step guide for the person preparing the prayer. It goes through all the details that need to be considered in order to prepare the prayer well.

Some of the texts gathered here were composed by ourselves, some we have taken from others, some we have reworked from other sources. Needless to say, while each of the prayer texts is self-contained, groups may wish to use or combine elements from different texts in their own ways. Hopefully, use of the book will help all who draw on it to become more creative with prayer

The origins of the book lie in our experience over a number of years with groups engaged in renewal in their parishes. This experience has confirmed again and again the fundamental importance of prayer for the group. When prayer *is* the heart of the work, the work itself is qualitatively different. The group experiences itself and what it does at a new depth. It is prayer, above all else, that leads the group into the mystery of God that is at the heart of what they do.

We extend thanks to our fellow workers in parish renewal over the years, for their witness to the importance of prayer, as well as for coming up with some of the resources gathered here. Thanks in particular to the other co-ordinators of parish renewal in Dublin – to Micheal Comer, Eilis O'Malley, Brid Liston, Tim Hurley and Oonagh O'Brien – for their help and support in bringing this book to completion.

Julie Kavanagh, Donal Harrington
Summer 1998

Praying Together
The Heartbeat of Every Parish Group

Experience has shown that prayer is at the heart of parish renewal and at the heart of all that parish groups do. Putting it simply, the parish group for which prayer is a vital element of its meetings is a group that flourishes in all that it does, through both success and failure.

However, fruitful and effective prayer in the parish group is often hampered by one or more of the following obstacles:

(a) a feeling of incompetence or inadequacy; the group wants to pray together and appreciates the value of prayer, but does not know how to go about it;

(b) misconceptions or conflicting conceptions within the group as to what prayer is. For instance, prayer means saying the rosary/or prayer means deep contemplation with long silences/or prayer means very personal sharing;

(c) the attitude that giving ten or fifteen minutes to prayer out of a meeting lasting one-and-a-half to two hours is equivalent to ten or fifteen minutes of precious meeting time lost. Let us look at these one by one.

From Feeling Apprehensive to Feeling Confident

This first obstacle is about a group feeling incompetent and inadequate about praying as a group. It is likely that behind these feelings of incompetence or inadequacy lie other issues. One such issue is that of leadership. Who leads the prayer in the group? Is it the priest, or the parish sister, or a local catechist? Or is it any one of us who is baptised? This question of leadership is an important one. Often a group will just presume that it is up to the priest or sister in the group. Even to suggest the possibility of other people leading prayer may be a very new idea for some. But it is an idea very much worth exploring.

No one person in a group is more qualified to lead prayer than another. Many groups rotate the leadership of the prayer and have found this to be a very positive experience. Before a group decides to rotate or widen the leadership of prayer, it is wise to give some time to discussing why the group might choose to do this and the apprehensions that group members may have.

Apprehensions that members of parish groups have shared include the following:

- *What do I say? Where do I start?*
- *I don't know any prayers or have any ideas/books/resources.*
- *The idea of preparing prayer is new to me.*
- *The pressure of having to produce the best prayer yet!*
- *It's the priest's job.*
- *What theme will I choose and will it be relevant to the group?*
- *How long/short should it be? What shape should it take?*
- *Perhaps only some people have the gift of leading prayer.*
- *I'm afraid of making a mess of it and making a fool of myself.*
- *How do I measure what the group can take without putting them off?*
- *Fear of people in the group and what they might think of me.*
- *People may be resistant to prayer or think that we are wasting time.*
- *Prayer is meant to be private.*
- *What if there is tension or conflict in the group?*

Obviously these are very real apprehensions. Experience has shown that it is wise and helpful to discuss them as a group before expanding prayer and its leadership within the group. One suggestion would be to use this chapter as something the whole group might read as a basis for discussion about prayer in the group.

However one does it, it is important to explore these fears and apprehensions. Some of the above apprehensions are about the perceived group attitude to a prayer leader. These can be relieved quite easily if acknowledged and discussed as a group, ahead of time.

As regards the actual content and conducting of the group's prayer, the material in this book, both in this introduction and in the actual resources, is designed to help each member of a parish group become competent in preparing and leading a time of prayer.

Groups where the prayer leadership is rotated have already begun to identify and affirm the positive aspects of such an approach. Their comments include the following:

- *Each person brings his/her own personality and colour to the prayer.*
- *Prayer is now more accessible.*
- *Prayer is as important, if not more important, than any other aspect of the meeting.*
- *It's okay to have a different style of prayer – there is no rigid formula.*
- *Leading prayer is not about being a priest or sister.*
- *Prayer is now at the centre of who we are and what we are about, it is not a frill or a necessary thing to go through before getting to the 'meeting'.*
- *More confidence to ground our work in our prayer and the gospel.*
- *I feel less embarrassed to talk about God and faith.*
- *Prayer is about more than saying words; trying to bring words and images to life.*
- *We've grown in our prayer together – it is freer and less fearful.*
- *It is good to see other people lead prayer.*
- *I think that we are more patient and listen to one another better because of our experience of prayer and the fact that we all own it, through shared leadership.*
- *I enjoy preparing the prayer and thinking about it beforehand. I also appreciate the work that goes into it when others do it.*

Prayer Means Different Things

Obstacle (b) was about misconceptions or conflicting perceptions within the group as to what prayer is. Prayer is, quite simply, making space to communicate with God. It is about setting aside a time and a place where we can consciously enter into God's presence. It is about creating a space in which we can both listen to and talk to God.

Prayer can take a variety of forms. It can consist of 'saying prayers', such as the rosary. It can consist of becoming quite still and maintaining an uninterrupted silence. It can consist of reflective reading of the Bible. It can involve singing and music. It can involve movement and dance. It can be indoors or outdoors. It can be alone or together, or a mixture of both.

In a parish group setting, prayer will tend to be more communal than personal, though time is often given for personal prayer. As a group, we create a space to welcome God into the heartbeat of our work.

Whatever form it takes, the essence of prayer is always the same – making space so as to be in communication with God. This does not mean that God is only there when we are praying. In fact, God is there all the time and most of us are probably 'praying' in an unconscious kind of way a lot of the time.

But when we make a special space for prayer, we become more keenly aware of the God who is there all the time. We realise that God speaks to us through the events of our lives and in the events of the lives of those around us. We meet God in the very 'stuff' of our lives – indeed this 'stuff' is the 'raw material' of our prayer! Prayer does not take us away from life; it brings us deeper into life.

The conversation that is prayer – ourselves and God, listening and speaking – changes us. It changes our hearts and then our lives. Prayer affirms and encourages us in our struggles, while it can also invite us to conversion and a change of heart. Either way, it makes a difference to how we live our lives.

The Importance of Prayer – Our Sharing in God's Work

Obstacle (c) above was about the feeling that prayer takes up precious time. People involved in parish groups have only so much time to give to meetings, maybe only an hour or two every month. Ten or fifteen minutes of prayer can look like a huge chunk taken out of a busy agenda. And yet, prayer is the one element in the work of a parish group that is indispensable.

There are many elements that make up the meeting – the initial chat, looking over minutes, debating issues, hearing reports, making decisions, input, small group discussions, planning, the cup of tea. Any one of these might be missing and the loss could be made up. But if there is no prayer, the group has lost sight of what it is about.

Nothing could be further from the truth than thinking that prayer time is lost time. The time given to prayer together is what gives the group its identity. This is not something that can be achieved with a cursory prayer at the start or the end of a meeting.

The reason for giving quality time to prayer lies in the nature of parish renewal. Whether the group is a leadership group or a ministry group within the parish, its work is contributing to renewal in the parish. And the work of parish renewal is the Lord's work, or rather our collaboration with God's saving work amongst us. Our efforts to share responsibility and collaborate with one another may sometimes obscure the more important fact that, in parish renewal, God is sharing responsibility with us. God is inviting us to become partners in the divine task of transforming all things in Christ.

The place of prayer in the life of the parish group is not unlike the place of the avowal of love in a relationship. If love is not spoken, if a couple do not frequently avow their love, that love will begin to dissolve. Likewise, in prayer the members of the group avow the love that inspires them. They name who they are. They declare aloud the Christianity that is the core of their humanity.

So, if prayer is lost everything is lost. The work becomes simply our work. As the psalmist declared, 'If the Lord does not build the house, in vain do the builders labour.' Without prayer the group might work efficiently, but the work will cease to be truly 'Christian'.

The Fruits of Prayer

Prayer is the gateway into a world where God and humankind strive together to build the kingdom. In prayer, parish group members open themselves to something that is greater than themselves. They open themselves to a divine-human collaboration that will bear rich fruit for them as a group. Reflecting on groups who actively place prayer at their centre, the following fruits can be identified:

Prayer unites the group in a single spirit. With their varied life experiences, members of the group each bring their own colour and spirit to the group's prayer. Though all can be in very different places in their lives, feeling different emotions, prayer makes it possible for all to be in the same place for a period of time.

Prayer helps the group focus on their vision and purpose. It brings them back to who they are and what they are about. A lot of activity can have the effect of 'scattering' a person. Prayer helps us to 'collect' ourselves again and to recover a sense of our overall direction.

Prayer provides a setting in which members of the group can share both their hopes and anxieties about the work of parish renewal and their own ministry. The sharing of uncertainties and convictions, of struggles and hopes, brings a new depth of relationship within the group.

Prayer yields a perspective on the highs and lows of the group's experience. It nurtures a proper appreciation of both success and failure, by placing both in the context of the Lord's slow work amongst us. It teaches the group to be less anxious about 'doing' and achieving and to be more aware of 'being' in a particular way, as a group who identify themselves as followers of Christ.

Prayer is both comforting and challenging. When members of the group are downhearted, prayer puts them back in touch with what they really want. It regenerates motivation and commitment. On the other

hand, when members grow complacent or self-congratulatory, it presents anew the challenge of renewal.

Clearly, the pulse of prayer within these groups nurtures and fosters their sense of partnership with God. Its constant presence as a heartbeat acts as a loving and gentle reminder of what the group is really about in any work undertaken in the name of the Church.

Some Suggestions for Starting Out

As a parish group sets out to make prayer an essential element of their time together, it may be helpful to keep in mind the following four suggestions:
   (a) Prepare well.
   (b) Move forward gently.
   (c) Aim for the participation of all.
   (d) Review the experience.

Prepare Well

Prayer need not be a complicated affair. But because it is so important, it should be carefully and lovingly prepared. There are tools to help us in our preparation. One set of tools is the collection of prayer texts that make up most of this book. Another set of tools is the guidelines that follow in the next chapter about how to use these prayer texts. To make the best use of the prayer texts you will need to use the guidelines!

This book, therefore, presumes the necessity of good preparation, done ahead of time with plenty of opportunity for thought and reflection on the part of those preparing and leading the prayer.

In practical terms, achieving good preparation means making sure that the person preparing the prayer has been given plenty of notice. It also means making sure that he/she has been given the above-mentioned tools to help them in the task.

Again, as has already been stated here, what is provided in this book is the text for prayer. The task of those preparing and leading prayer is to transform a text for prayer into an experience of prayer. This can only be done through careful preparation.

Move Forward Gently

Group prayer may be new to many parish group members. It is very important that the prayer time be a positive, non-threatening experience from the beginning. This means starting with very straightforward prayer, where most of the focus is on using the text and not too much focus is on silence or spontaneous shared prayer.

As time goes on, and the group becomes more familiar with the format, the prayer can become more imaginative – with more attention to the sacred space, more time for silence, more sharing of personal reflections and prayers. Also, as time goes on, the time for prayer may expand; it should never be less than ten minutes, but it may sometimes come to take up twice this time or more.

Aim for the Participation of All

This means two things. First, the prayer should allow for maximum participation, through sharing out prayers and readings (or sections of readings) and through time for spontaneous prayer. Second, the preparation and leadership of the prayer should be rotated around the group. In the initial stages, members might find it less intimidating if they prepared the prayer in pairs.

A simple yet vital way of helping to maximise participation is to make sure that everyone in the group has a copy of the prayer text. In practical terms this means photocopying the material to be used. Although it may be troublesome, the usefulness of ensuring that everyone has a copy of the prayer cannot be exaggerated. It means that members have the texts to ponder during times of quiet reflection and for any spoken responses they might have in the prayer. It also enables members to take home the prayer and to use it themselves, privately or with their families.

Review the Experience

It is advisable to check in occasionally with the group as to how the experience of prayer is for members. By doing such a check-in, any tensions or concerns about the prayer and its leadership can be raised. It also gives members an opportunity to share what they have experienced as the fruits or benefits of prayer in the group.

By engaging in an occasional review of the prayer within the group, the group remains attentive to how they go about prayer. It is not taken for granted, but can be continually reflected upon and enriched.

Preparing a Prayer Session
A Step-by-Step Guide

Again, as has already been stated, what is provided in this book is the text for prayer. The task of those preparing and leading prayer is to transform the text for prayer into an experience of prayer. The following guidelines are offered with this task in mind.

Step One: Note the Elements of Group Prayer

Obviously there is more to prayer than simply the text we use. Before preparing and leading group prayer, it is important to note the variety of elements that it includes. The following are those elements. They are flexible and need not all be present on each occasion. Their sequence can be adapted.

The Setting
The Sacred Space
The Introduction and Focusing
Music
Reading(s) and/or Reflection(s)
Movement/Gesture
Quiet Time/Silence
Shared Prayer/Reflections
Intercessions
Concluding Prayer

Some of these elements may be very new to group members. When looked at more closely, each of them can be seen to be quite straightforward.

The Setting
A key to deepening the experience of prayer is attending to mood and

atmosphere, which is created by the setting. If people are merely rattling off a perfunctory prayer, the setting is inconsequential. If they want prayer to be what it can be, setting is all important. Setting includes the lighting, heating and seating arrangement of the room.

Prayer is often enhanced by dim lighting (while making sure that readers can read their sheets), and is most certainly enhanced by a warm environment. If a room is too hot or too cold, people will not want to linger in prayer. Ideally people should be seated in a circle or semi-circle, and the seating should be comfortable but firm. Sitting in rows, or in uncomfortable chairs, will not help the experience of prayer.

The Sacred Space

The sacred space refers to a central, visual, focus for the group. It reminds the group of the presence of the Lord among them. It may be as simple as a lighted candle placed in the middle of the floor or table. It may be more elaborate, including, for instance, cloth, flowers, leaves/branches, icon/painting, photographs. What is chosen for the sacred space will depend on the images within the text of prayer, and/or on the time or season of the year.

As a year unfolds, the following visual ideas or themes might suggest themselves:

Early Autumn: first fruits, abundance, harvest, green, darker emerald green ...

Late October/November: green, natural browns/rusts, berries, natural rough fabrics, dry leaves, wheat, pumpkins, lanterns, prayers for the dead ...

Advent: violet, blue – royal and lighter shades in contrast, silver, barren, deciduous branches, advent wreath, Jesse tree ...

Christmas: Light, white, poinsettias, evergreens, richness of fabric, gold, green, red ...

January/Spring: green, snowdrops, new beginnings, fresh start, new life, first hints of new growth, bulbs, buds, daffodils, St Brigid ...

Lent: purple, browns, ashes, barrenness, water jugs, sand, desert, stones ...

March: St Patrick, green, heritage, water, baptism, holy sites …
Easter: white, bursts of colour, primary colours, flowers (lily, tulips, mums …) richness in smell and sight, oil, light, renewal, rebirth, water …
May: Mary, Pentecost, blooming flowers, red, dove, spirit, wind, life …
Summer: green, yellows, plants, flowers, …

The Introduction and Focusing

The very manner in which the prayer begins is vital. What happens at the beginning sets the tone for what is to follow. The leader, therefore, will need to give some thought to how they will begin. He/she may decide to introduce the prayer. This may include mentioning the theme of the prayer and giving the outline of the prayer. The first words spoken by the leader are key and require some thought and care ahead of time.

Focusing refers to the time at the beginning of the prayer where people gather themselves and settle down into a spirit of prayer. This might involve the prayer leader allowing a few moments quiet for people to focus on the theme. It might be appropriate to play some music and/or to slowly read the focus text on the prayer sheet, if there is one.

The leader might invite people to make the sign of the cross, before or after the focusing time.

Music

Music can enhance the prayer experience, by embellishing the theme or by helping people to enter into a time of reflection. It can be used at a variety of stages within the prayer, depending on what it is being used for. It can be instrumental or sung. If using a tape recorder or CD player, this will have to be set beforehand and the leader will need to know when to start and stop it. Some groups may have a repertoire of hymns/songs that they can sing themselves.

Reading(s) and/or Reflection(s)

The readings and reflections within these resources come from a variety of sources, including scripture. Readings and reflections are not hurried elements of prayer. They need to be slowly and carefully read, with plenty of time for pauses.

Movement/ Gesture

Depending on the content and context of the prayer, the group may be invited to do such things as light a candle, pick up and hold one of the symbols from the sacred space, share a sign of peace, or stand. Part of the prayer preparation is deciding if and how the element of movement/ gesture will be included.

Quiet Time /Silence

Silence is something with which many of us feel uncomfortable. However, it is a very necessary element within prayer. It is so necessary, in fact, that without silence our prayer is weakened. If we have no silence how will we hear God speaking to us?

Because the leader may feel a sense of responsibility for the group's prayer, he/she may in fact be more uncomfortable with silence than other members of the group. The silence may feel longer or more tension-filled than it actually is. The leader may sense a restlessness within the group that in reality is not there. As a prayer leader, the leader should try to grow more and more comfortable with silence where it is appropriate and not rush along too quickly.

Shared Prayer/Reflections

This is another element of prayer that may be new and fearful for some members of the group. Nobody should ever feel that they have to share either a prayer or their own reflections on what has been read or experienced in the prayer. Such sharing should come freely from members.

When leading the prayer and inviting any sharing from the group, it is important to do so in a non-threatening manner. Do not be discouraged if people are slow to share their prayer/reflections. As time goes on, the group will do so more readily.

Often a leader will find that there may be a significant silence before the first person shares a prayer/reflection. Then a number of other people may share quite quickly. The prayer leader needs to be patient during this initial silence and to resist the temptation to move on to the next element of prayer. When another significant silence emerges from the group it may then be time to move on.

Some of the prayer texts in this booklet have specific intercessions within them and these may be ample for that particular prayer session.

 # Intercessions
When provided, the intercessions normally have a response for the group. The prayer leader may choose to lead these intercessions or to delegate a member of the group to do so.

 # Concluding Prayer
The concluding prayer might be said by the leader. Alternatively, he/she might invite everybody to join in saying it together. If the prayer has begun with a sign of the cross, the leader invites people to bring it to a close with the same gesture.

Step Two: Select a Text for the Prayer

The next step is to select a text for the prayer. When doing this, it is helpful to reflect on the group who will be praying together. Perhaps there is a particular theme that would be good for the group to explore at this time. The theme might also be decided upon in light of the season in nature or in the Church year.

Step Three: Work with the Text

As has been said, choosing the text is just the beginning of the preparation! The next step is to read the text carefully and enter into it. The questions on page 26 are designed as a guide to help those preparing and leading the prayer to engage in such a process of entering in.

It may be useful for the leader to photocopy these questions and use them as a worksheet for his/her preparation.

Once these questions have been explored, the leader will have a better sense of the spirit of the prayer, while also knowing what practical preparations are needed for it.

Step Four: Use the following checklist for the final stage of preparation

- Arrive early to allow plenty of time to set-up.
- Attend to the setting, making sure that the lighting, heating and seating arrangement will enhance rather than impede group prayer.
- Create the sacred space.
- If using taped music, have the music set and check that the machine works!
- Delegate the tasks within the prayer to other members of the group.
- Distribute the prayer sheets to the group and introduce the prayer.
- Once the prayer begins, trust and let go. And let the Spirit work!

GUIDING QUESTIONS FOR EXPLORING THE SELECTED PRAYER TEXT

1. What is the mood and message of the prayer?

2. What images do you find in the text?

3. What symbols suggest themselves for the sacred space (fabrics, colours, oils, incense, icons, branches, rocks, etc.)?

4. Is there any piece of music that the text suggests?

5. Are there any particular gestures or movements/actions that might form part of the prayer experience?

6. What tasks (e.g. readings, sections of reading) are there to delegate to others in the group, so as to maximise participation?

7. What will you say by way of introducing the prayer and focusing people at the beginning?

8. Where will there be pauses for silence?

9. Will you tell the readers when to begin or will they decide themselves?

10. If there is to be a concluding prayer at the end of meeting, might you use some element from this text?

11. Will every one have a copy of the prayer?

Small Beginnings

Focusing

Scripture

The kingdom of heaven is like a mustard seed
that someone took and sowed in his field;
it is the smallest of all the seeds,
but when it has grown it is the greatest of shrubs
and becomes a tree, so that the birds of the air come
and make nests in its branches.
(Matthew 13:31-32)

Reflection

Many if not all great undertakings
begin in small and often hidden ways.
Seeds need the darkness, isolation and cover of the earth
in order to germinate.
Therefore, for something to begin small, hidden, anyonymous,
is an advantage.
It means it can develop away from publicity.
There are no pressures. No burden of expectations.
It can develop at its own pace. There is no hurry.
Hurry ruins so many things.
Hence the importance of beginnings,
of taking care of things in their beginning,
of the small in the accomplishment of the great.

How did Christ begin his great work, the salvation of the world?
He began simply, quietly. No fanfare. No fireworks. No public launching.
He began by calling a few people – two in fact.
It was as simple as that.
He began with personal contact
and that is how his work developed.
It was passed on from person to person by word of mouth.

We shouldn't be surprised at this.
Things which begin with a splash often peter out.
Whereas those which begin quietly put down deep roots,
grow steadily, and survive to produce fruits that last.

So, if there is something which we want to do,
let us not hesitate and think too much.
Let us make a start, however small.
Let us take one step. Let us plant one seed.
Let us trust that if our cause is good,
God will support us, and it will grow and prosper.[1]

Quiet Prayer

Shared Reflections/Prayers

Concluding Prayer
O God of small beginnings,
fill us with confidence in our work.
May your presence in what we do encourage us to dare.
May solidarity and togetherness be our strength.

---

1. Flor McCarthy, *Windows on the Gospel* (Dublin: Dominican Publications, 1992), 38-40

Instruments of God

Focusing

Reflection

> A small wooden flute,
> an empty, hollow reed,
> rests in her silent hand.
>
> it awaits the breath
> of one who creates song
> through its open form.
>
> my often-empty life
> rests in the hand of God;
> like the hollowed flute,
> it yearns for the melody
> which only Breath can give.
>
> the small wooden flute and I,
> we need the one who breathes,
> we await one who makes melody.
>
> and the one whose touch creates,
> awaits our empty, ordinary forms,
> so that the song-starved world
> may be fed with golden melodies.[2]

Quiet Time

A Litany of Being God's Instruments of Goodness

Response: God who sings through us, we thank you.

For the talents and the abundance of gifts that are ours...

For the faith that stirs and grows in our hearts...

For the many people who have been instruments of your goodness in our lives...

For the moments when we have heard the song of your presence in our lives...

For the times when your goodness has made music through us...

Response: God of goodness, help us to trust you.

When fear rises up in us and we do not believe in ourselves as your instruments...

When busy-ness and pressures lead us to lose the sense of your song within us...

When we doubt your presence in the difficult aspects of our day...

When emptiness, loneliness and other struggles block out your melody of love...

Response: God of love, sing your song through us.

As we grow in believing in our goodness...

As we allow more and more of ourselves to be influenced by your presence...

As the call to be your instruments becomes clearer to us...

As we seek to discern how and when to share our goodness with others...[3]

Shared Prayer

Closing Prayer

Glory be to God, whose power working in us
can do infinitely more than we can ever ask or imagine.

---

2. Joyce Rupp, *May I Have this Dance?* (Notre Dame: Ave Maria Press, 1992), 117
3. Joyce Rupp, *May I Have this Dance?* 125-6 (adapted)

That Dreams would Soar

Focusing

Scripture

For it is as if a man, going on a journey, summoned his slaves and entrusted his property to them; to one he gave five talents, to another two, to another one, to each according to their ability. Then he went away. The one who had received the five talents went off at once and traded with them and made five more talents. In the same way, the one who had the two talents made two more talents. But the one who had received the one talent went off and dug a hole in the ground and hid his master's money. *(Matthew 25:14-18)*

Meditation

Dreams come and go in our lives;
far more die than come to reality.
What is it in us that allows us to let go of visions
that could create new and beautiful worlds?
Why do we so easily give in to barriers?
Why do we let ourselves conform and be satisfied with what is?
Reaching out to a dream can be risky.
It can involve hardships that our imaginations never knew.
Our comfortableness can so easily be disturbed.
But, what beauty can be exerienced
as we accept the challenge of a dream!
What a precious feeling to be supported, to have others say
'You can do it, we can do it together.'
Nothing is beyond our reach if we reach out together,
if we reach out with all the confidence we have,

if we are willing to persevere even in difficult times
and if we rejoice with every small step forward,
if we dream beautiful dreams
that will transform our lives, our world.
Nothing is impossible if we put aside our careful ways,
if we build our dreams with faith —
faith in ourselves,
faith in our sisters and brothers,
and above all,
faith in our Lord God
with whom all things are possible.[4]

Quiet Prayer

Shared Reflections/Intercessions

Concluding Prayer

We pray to you, God of heaven and earth,
in wonder and thanks
that you have reached out to us,
dreaming and risking.
We pray through your Son Jesus who,
never satisfied with what is,
endured hardships the mind could not anticipate.
We pray in your Spirit,
released into the world by your dream for us,
who teaches us that nothing is beyond our collective reach.
May your Spirit inspire us
with the confidence not to bury our talents,
but to give ourselves unreservedly to the dreams
that will transform our lives.

---

4 Delora Hintz, *Prayer Services for Parish Meetings* (Mystic CT: Twenty-Third Publications, 1983), 66-67

Stones

Focusing

Let us bow our heads before the wonder of creation ... 'In the beginning God created the heavens and the earth ...' 'In the beginning was the Word; the Word was with God, and the Word was God ... through him all things came to be; not one thing had its being but through him.'

A variety of stones are placed on an ornamental cloth with reverence – it is God who made them. 'And God saw that it was good.'

Reflection

The variety of stones.

God made stones in great variety ... variety of shapes, circular and irregular ... variety of sizes, small and larger ... variety of textures, smooth and porous ... variety of colours ... *Pause ...*
O God of variety, save us from monotony and sameness. Lord hear us.

The variety of uses of stones

God's people in their creativity have discovered a variety of uses for stones ... corner stones ... foundation stones ... millstones ... stepping stones ... headstones ... wall stones ... ornamental stones ... paving stones ... and fun stones (the Blarney stone, the stone outside Dan Murphy's door). *Pause ...*
Creator God, you made us in your image. You also made us of the same stuff as the stones. May our creativity show forth your creativity which you have so strikingly revealed to us.
Lord hear us.

Stones and time

Celebrating two thousand years of Christianity ... placing this in the context of the stones on the table, five hundred million years in existence. *Pause ...*

Lord God, we reflect on the immensity of time and space,
of stone and of all creation.
May the immensity that is you not overwhelm us,
but lift our hearts in wonder and humility. Lord hear us.

Stones in Scripture

Yahweh said to Moses: 'Come up to me on the mountain and stay there.
I will give you the slabs of stone, the Teaching and Commandments
which I have written for their instruction.' *Pause ...*
Liberating God, may we see your commandments as your gift to us,
a path to life, signs of your love and care,
leading to blessedness as we take on your ways. Lord hear us.

Jesus and stones

'Let the one who is without sin cast the first stone.' *Pause ...*
Lord, let me see that if I cast the first stone or any stone,
then I have become that stone. Lord hear us.

'Which of you would give your son a stone when he asked for bread?'
Pause ...
Lord, we turn to you for nourishment, you who are the Bread of Life.
Lord hear us.

'Some seed fell on stoney ground.' *Pause ...*
Lord, may we keep searching for ways to prepare the soil
so that your Word will bear fruit a hundredfold. Lord hear us.

Concluding Prayer

Each take a stone from the centre, contemplating quietly with the words,
'They found the stone had been rolled away.' Then say together:
Lord, we ask your help, that we leave no stone unturned,
as we continue to roll away the stones that entomb us.
Then we can rise with you. Amen.[5]

---

5 Composed by Donal O'Doherty (printed with permission)

A Disciple's Heart

When you were born,
you cried and the world rejoiced.
Live your life in such a manner that,
when you die,
the world cries and you rejoice.

Focusing

Scripture

Be dressed for action and have your lamps lit;
be like those who are waiting for their master
to return from the wedding banquet,
so that they may open the door for him
as soon as he comes and knocks.
Blessed are those slaves
whom the master finds alert when he comes;
truly I tell you, he will fasten his belt
and have them sit down to eat,
and he will come and serve them.
If he comes during the middle of the night,
or near dawn, and finds them so,
blessed are those slaves.
(Luke 12:35-38)

Meditation

> *Lord of the winds, I cry to Thee,*
> *I that am dust,*
> *And blown about by every gust*
> *I fly to Thee.*
>
> *Lord of the waters, upon Thee I call.*
> *I that am weed upon the waters borne,*
> *And by the waters torn,*
> *Tossed by the waters, at Thy feet I fall.*
> *(Mary Coleridge)*

Pause for Reflection

Time for Sharing

Concluding Prayer

We bless you Lord for our calling
for nurturing in each of us a disciple's heart
a heart that rejoices in your coming
a heart sustained by your Spirit
a heart encouraged by fellow disciples.
May there grow in each of our hearts
the disciple's commitment to serve
the disciple's willingness to learn
and the disciple's joy in becoming
a medium of your grace.

We Believe

We rest from our work, our activity
to make contact again
with the fire that burns within us
the passion of our faith
the conviction of what we believe in.

Focusing

A Creed

We believe in God
who did not create an immutable world, a thing incapable of change;
who does not govern according to eternal laws that remain inviolate,
or according to a natural order of rich and poor,
of the expert and the ignorant, of rulers and subjects.

We believe in God
who willed conflict in life
and wanted us to change the status quo
through our work, through our politics.

We believe in Jesus Christ
who was right when he, like each of us,
just another individual who couldn't beat city hall,
worked to change the status quo, and was destroyed.
Looking at him I see how our intelligence is crippled,
our imagination stifled, our efforts wasted
because we do not live as he did.
Every day I am afraid that he died in vain
because he is buried in our churches,
because we have betrayed his revolution
in our obedience to authority and our fear of it.

We believe in Jesus Christ
who rises again and again in our lives
so that we will be free
from prejudice and arrogance, from fear and hate,
and carry on his revolution
and make way for his kingdom.
We believe in the Spirit that Jesus brought into the world.
We believe it is up to us what our earth becomes,
a vale of tears, starvation and tyranny,
or a city of God.

We believe in a just peace that can be achieved,
in the possibility of a meaningful life for all people.
We believe this world of God's has a future. Amen.[6]

Quiet Prayer

Shared Reflections/Prayers

Closing Prayer

The love of God flowing free
The love of God flow out through me.
The peace of God flowing free
The peace of God flow out through me.
The life of God flowing free
The life of God flow out through me.[7]

---

6 Dorothy Sölle, *Revolutionary Patience* (Maryknoll: Orbis Books), (adapted)
7 David Adam, *Tides and Seasons* (London: SPCK Triangle, 1989), 51

Sing a New Song to the Lord

*There is no more difference between
the written gospels and the lives of saints
than between written music and music sung.
(Francis de Sales)*

Focusing

Scripture

The seventy returned with joy, saying,
'Lord, in your name even the demons submit to us!'
He said to them,
'I watched Satan fall from heaven like a flash of lightning.
See, I have given you authority to tread on snakes and scorpions,
and over all the power of the enemy; and nothing will hurt you.
Nevertheless, do not rejoice at this, that the spirits submit to you,
but rejoice that your names are written in heaven.'
(Luke 10:17-20)

Quiet Prayer

*In this quiet time, thank God that our names are written in heaven;
praise God for the ways in which our lives sing forth the gospel.*

Reflection

'Sing to the Lord a new song, his praise in the assembly of the faithful.'
We are told to sing to the Lord a new song. A new person knows a new
song. A song is a thing of joy and, if we think carefully about it, a thing
of love. So the one who has learned to love a new life has learned to sing
a new song. And a new person, a new song and a new testament all
belong to the same kingdom.

My children, holy seeds of heaven, you who have been born again in Christ, born from above, 'sing to the Lord a new song'. 'But I do sing', you may say. You sing, of course you sing ... but make sure that your life sings the same tune as your mouth. Sing with your voices, sing with your hearts, sing with your lips, sing with your lives ... The singer himself or herself is the praise contained in the song ... Do you want to speak the praise of God? Be yourselves what you speak. If you live good lives, you are his praise. *(Augustine, Sermon 34)*

Intercessions

Thank God for people through whose lives we hear the gospel sung, in whom we hear God praised.

Concluding Prayer

Come Lord Jesus and sing your song in us
    — that we may live the truth we sing.
Show us the path of life and reveal your justice to the nations
    — that we may live the truth we sing.
Gently bring us to ways of compassion
    — that we may live the truth we sing.
Fill our hearts with the power of your love
    — that we may live the truth we sing.
Guide our actions by the light of grace
    — that we may live the truth we sing.
Bless us and sustain us in the name of the Trinity
    — that we may live the truth we sing.

Bread of the Kingdom

Focusing

Reflection

'Far from diminishing our concern to develop this earth,
the expectation of a new earth should spur us on,
for it is here that the body of a new human family grows,
foreshadowing in some way the age which is to come.
That is why earthly progress
is of vital concern to the kingdom of God.
When we have nurtured on earth the values
of human dignity, communion and freedom,
we will find them once again,
freed from stain, illuminated and transfigured.
Here on earth the kingdom is mysteriously present;
when the Lord comes, it will enter into its perfection.'
(Vatican II, The Church in the Modern World, 39)

The Song of the Bread

Bread from seed sown in earth
bread made by human hands
bread tasting of sorrow
and of people of many lands

bread of war and of peace
unchanging daily bread
strange bread of affection
and the stone bread of the dead

bread, our body our all
earned with such bitter sweat
bread, life with our fellows
whom we easily forget

bread without which we die
matter of such great worth
bread shared with each other
through all our life on earth.

Bread of life shared with us –
you give yourself as food
you, man among others
and a God of flesh and blood.[8]

Quiet Prayer

Shared Reflections/Intercessions

Concluding Prayer

Lord our God, you have sown in us your word,
given us your son – he, who was broken and died for us,
is bread and life for the world.
We ask you to let us find strength to tread his path,
to let us be for each other as fertile as seed and as nourishing as bread
and thus lead a happy life.[9]

---

8 Huub Oosterhuis, *Your Word is Near* (New York: Paulist, 1968), 138
9 Huub Oosterhuis, *Your Word is Near,* 139

A Prayer on our Journey

Focusing

Leader: Let us pray to the God who supports and nourishes us along the path of life. Let us thank God for the signs of care and loving providence that we find so reassuring along the way.

All: God of hope, accompany us along the way.

Scripture

The whole congregation of the Israelites came to the wilderness of Sin. And they complained against Moses and Aaron, 'If only we had died by the hand of the Lord in the land of Egypt, when we sat by the fleshpots and ate our fill of bread; for you have brought us out into this wilderness to kill this whole assembly with hunger.'

Then the Lord said to Moses, 'I am going to rain bread from heaven for you, and each day the people shall go out and gather enough for that day. In that way I will test them, whether they will follow my instruction or not.'

Moses and Aaron said to all the Israelites, 'In the evening you shall know that it was the Lord who brought you out of the land of Egypt, and in the morning you shall see the glory of the Lord, because he has heard your complaining against the Lord. For what are we, that you complain against us?'

Then Moses said to Aaron, 'Say to the whole congregation of the Israelites, "Draw near to the Lord, for he has heard your complaining".' And as Aaron spoke to the whole congregation of the Israelites, they looked towards the wilderness, and the glory of the Lord appeared in the cloud. *(Exodus 16:1-10)*

Quiet Prayer

Intercessions

In the fear and apprehension in the hesitation and insecurity that we
experience as we follow you ...
God of hope, accompany us along the way.

In the sense of mystery, in the wonder that dawns in us,
as we seek to follow you ...
God of hope, accompany us along the way.

In the expectation and pain and restlessness that we experience
as we follow you ...
God of hope, accompany us along the way.

When we grow tired and weary, when the burden makes us falter
and want to stop ...
God of hope, accompany us along the way.

When we grow in insight, as your wisdom prompts us when to let go
and when to take up ...

God of hope, accompany us along the way.

When we glimpse your presence and thrill to the sense of your nearness ...
God of hope, accompany us along the way.

Concluding Prayer

God of hope,
like the people of Israel, we also complain,
we too need to learn.
Enliven in us the memory of how you have released us from bondage.
Teach us to rest secure in your presence accompanying us on the way.
Inspire us to acknowledge the signs of hope
and to respond to the invitations to new life
that we find along the way.

In Silence, Peace

Sometimes in a lonely cell
in the presence of my God
I stand and listen.
In the silence of my heart
I can hear God's will
when I listen.
For I am but a servant
who is guided by my king
when I listen.
(Columba)

Focusing

Reflection

To deliver oneself up, to hand oneself over, entrust oneself completely to the silence of a wide landscape of woods and hills, or seas, or desert, to sit still while the sun comes up over that land and fills its silences with light. To pray and work in the morning and to labour and rest in the afternoon, and to sit still again in meditation in the evening when night falls upon that land and when the silence fills itself with darkness and with stars. This is a true and special vocation.[10]

Quiet Prayer

Scripture: a Modern Version of Psalm 23

The Lord is my pace-setter, I shall not rush;
he makes me stop for quiet intervals.
He provides me with images of stillness
which restore my serenity.
He leads me in ways of efficiency through calmness of mind
and his guidance is peace.

Even though I have a great many things to accomplish each day
I will not fret, for his presence is here;
his timelessness, his all-importance will keep me in balance,
as he prepares refreshment and renewal in the midst of my activity.

When he anoints my mind with his oils of tranquillity,
my cup of joyous energy overflows.
Truly, harmony and effectiveness shall be the fruits of my hours,
for I shall walk in the pace of my Lord
and dwell in his house forever.
(Tokio Megashia)

Shared Reflections/Prayers

Concluding Prayer

We thank you, Lord, for your gift of silence –
for these moments now
and for the other silent spaces you give us during the day.
We thank you for the gift of yourself in silence,
and for the knowledge that you, whom we so easily neglect,
are so wonderfully close and alive in our lives. Amen.

---

10 Thomas Merton, *Thoughts in Solitude* (New York: Farrar, Strauss and Cudahy, 1956), 101

Beatitudes of Nature

Come Lord, come down,
Come in, come among us.
Come as the wind to move us,
Come as the light to prove us,
Come as the night to rest us,
Come as the storm to test us,
Come as the sun to warm us,
Come as the stillness to calm us,
Come Lord, come down,
Come in, come among us.[11]

Focusing

Beatitudes

Blessed is the tree which takes time to sink deep roots
– it shows us what we have to do in order to withstand the storm.

Blessed is the seed which falls on good soil and so produces a rich harvest
– it shows us what happens when we take the word of God to heart.

Blessed is the vine which, having been pruned, becomes all the more fruitful
– it shows us the benefit of self-denial.

Blessed are the flowers of the fields
– their beauty bears witness to God's prodigal artistry.

Blessed are the ubiquitous sparrows
– their carefree attitude to life gives us a lesson to trust in providence.

Blessed is the wind, coming from where we do not know,
to set sails in motion, to breathe life into dying embers
– it reminds us of the mysterious workings of the Spirit of God.

Blessed is the rain which falls without favour on all fields
– in it we see a reflection of God's indiscriminate love for all God's children.

Blessed are the leaves, which know when to let go,
and do so in a blaze of colour
– they show us how to die.[12]

Quiet Prayer

Shared Reflections/Prayers

Concluding Prayer
Praised be Jesus, in love with God
        and enraptured by all God's creation.
Praised be the imagination of Jesus,
        seeing in creation so much of God's wisdom.
Praised be Jesus for imaging to us,
        through creation, so much of life.
Praised be God's creation,
        speaking through Jesus to us.
Praised be our imaginations,
        vitalised by the words of Jesus.
Praised be God
        who makes all things possible.

---

11 David Adam, *Tides and Seasons*, 22
12 Flor McCarthy, *Windows on the Gospel*, 18-19

Hope, our Friend in Need

Focusing

Scripture

It is the God who said, 'Let light out of darkness,' who has shone in our hearts to give the light of the knowledge of the glory of God in the face of Jesus Christ. But we have this treasure in clay jars, so that it may be made clear that this extraordinary power belongs to God and does not come from us. We are afflicted in every way, but not crushed; perplexed, but not driven to despair; persecuted, but not forsaken; struck down, but not destroyed; always carrying in the body the death of Jesus, so that the life of Jesus may also be made visible in our bodies.
(2 Corinthians 4:6-10)

Hope

> *Even at the gates of hell,*
> *Believe in redemption.*
> *Let my grace and power work,*
> *Where you have none.*
> *It is only for you*
> *To believe and to trust.*
> *Be confident.*
> *Trust.*
> *Love.*
> *Do not condemn.*
> *Believe,*
> *In the face of unbelief.*
> *Hope against hope.*
> *This is faith.*

This is the gift most needed
For those who have suffered
So deeply, and lost all.
You must manifest love and hope.
It is only then
That my people will begin to
Believe in themselves.[13]

Quiet Time/Shared Prayer

Litany
Response: Spirit of hope, come to sustain us; Spirit of Christ, lift up our hearts.

Our progress is slow. At first we expect great things
and then we learn to appreciate small steps forward. *Response.*

Difficulties and adversity make our work feel frustrating.
But trusting in you, we want be part of the struggle. *Response.*

There is no blueprint, no neat solution –
yet in the messiness, we learn to see your hand. *Response.*

It's complicated when people are so different in their approaches.
We need to trust each other when conflict surfaces. *Response.*

Confusion and perplexity and searching characterise our work.
We thank you Lord for the light that urges us to keep going. *Response.*

In the pain of failure, Jesus touches our hearts.
He whose dying was the seed of new life
inspires us to envisage new beginnings. *Response.*

Blessed be God eternal, watching over all we do.
Blessed be Jesus our wisdom, companion in the striving.
Blessed be the divine Spirit, constantly renewing our hearts. Amen.

---

13 Edwina Gateley, *I Hear a Seed Growing* (Wheathampstead, Herts: Anthony Clark, 1990), 134

Called into Community

Focusing

Scripture

The body does not consist of one member but of many.
If the foot would say, 'Because I am not a hand, I do not belong to the body',
that would not make it any less a part of the body.
If the ear would say, 'Because I am not an eye, I do not belong to the body',
that would not make it any less a part of the body...
But as it is, God arranged the members of the body,
each one of them, as he chose.
If all were a single member, where would the body be?
As it is, there are many members, yet one body.
The eye cannot say to the hand, 'I have no need of you',
nor again the head to the feet, 'I have no need of you'.
On the contrary, the members of the body
that seem to be the weaker are indispensable,
and those members of the body that we consider less honourable
we clothe with greatest honour...
God has so arranged the body, giving the greater honour to the inferior member,
that there may be no dissension within the body,
but the members may have the same care for one another.
If one member suffers, all suffer together with it;
if one member is honoured, all rejoice together with it.
Now, you are the body of Christ and individually members of it.
(1 Corinthians 12:14-26)

Reflection and Sharing

Reflect on our tendency to undervalue our own giftedness and to think that our own potential contribution to building Christian community is not very significant. Make a mental list of the ways in which you are gifted. When all are ready, leave time for sharing and/or giving thanks for this giftedness.

Concluding Prayer

9/20/00 — RCIA

God our Father, in your loving providence
you have brought us into being
to find joy in communion with one another
and to know you in our joy.

We give you praise and thanks for the communion we share
as members of the Body of Christ your Son.
We give thanks for each member of the Body
particularly in our own parish community,
for friend and stranger, for the lucky and the unlucky,
for the ones on the fringes and for those near the centre.

Fill us, we pray, with the Spirit of your Son.
Give us confidence
as you call us to build up the Body of Christ.
Help us to see in our everyday lives
the moments and opportunities
for caring and confirming and reconciling.
Bless us with the patience to overcome frustration
and with hope as we journey together.

We ask this with confidence
in the love you have shown us
through Christ our Lord. Amen.

The Slow Work of God

Focusing

Scripture

He also said, 'The kingdom of God is as if
someone would scatter seed on the ground,
and would sleep and rise, night and day,
and the see would sprout and grow,
he does not know how.
The earth produces of itself, first the stalk,
then the head, then the full grain in the head.
But when the grain is ripe,
at once he goes in with his sickle,
because the harvest has come.' *(Mark 4:26-29)*

Meditation

Above all, trust in the slow work of God.
We are, quite naturally,
impatient in everything to reach the end without delay ...
We should like to skip the intermediate stages.
We are impatient of being on the way to something unknown,
something new.
And yet it is the law of all progress
that is is made by passing through some stages of instability ...
and that it may take a very long time.

And so I think it is with you.
Your ideas mature gradually;
let them grow, let them shape themselves,
without undue haste.

Don't try to force them on,
as though you could be today what time
(that is to say, grace and circumstances acting on your own goodwill)
will make you tomorrow.
Only God could say what this new spirit
gradually forming within you will be.
Give our Lord the benefit of your believing
that his hand is leading you,
and of your accepting the anxiety
of feeling yourself in suspense and incomplete.
(Teilhard deChardin)

Quiet Prayer

Shared Reflections/Prayers

Concluding Prayer
We thank you, Lord,
for our enthusiasm to get things done
and to achieve results.
We thank you for the energy of our commitment.

But we ask you, Lord,
to imbue our dedicated hearts
with a spirit of patience and endurance
that corresponds to the gradual way
in which your reign is realised among us.

May this patient spirit save us
from restlessness, agitation and frustration in our work
and yield in us instead the peace of heart
that frees us to see the fruits of your Spirit in our midst.

We ask this through Jesus your Son who,
in the power of the Spirit,
reigns at your right hand for ever and ever. Amen.

Change the World by Changing Me

Spirit of the living God, fall afresh on us,
Spirit of the living God, fall afresh on us,
Melt us, mould us, fill us, use us.
Spirit of the living God, fall afresh on us

Focusing

Scripture

Do not judge, so that you may not be judged. For with the judgment
you make you will be judged, and the measure you give will be the
measure you get. Why do you see the speck in your neighbour's eye, but
do not notice the log in your own eye? Or how can you say to your
neighbour, 'Let me take the speck out of your eye', while the log is in
your own eye? You hypocrite, first take the log out of your own eye, and
then you will see clearly to take the speck out of your neighbour's eye.
(Matthew 7:1-6)

Reflection

The Sufi Bayazid says this about himself: 'I was a revolutionary when I
was young and all my prayer to God was, "Lord give me the energy to
change the world."

As I approached middle age and realised that half my life was gone
without my changing a single soul, I changed my prayer to: "Lord, give
me the grace to change all those who come in contact with me. Just my
family and friends, and I shall be content."

Now that I am an old man and my days are numbered, my prayer now
is: "Lord, give me the grace to change myself." If I had prayed for this
right from the start I should not have wasted my life".'

*Everybody thinks of changing humanity. Hardly anyone thinks of changing
themselves.*[14]

Quiet Prayer / Shared Reflection

Intercessions

Disturb us, O Lord
when we are too well pleased with ourselves;
when our dreams have come true
because we dreamed too little;
when we have arrived in safety
because we sailed too close to the shore.

Disturb us, O Lord
when with the abundance of things we possess
we have lost our thirst for the waters of Life;
when, having fallen in love with time,
we have ceased to dream of eternity;
and when, in our efforts to build a new earth,
we have allowed our vision of the New Heaven to grow dim.

Stir us, O Lord to dare more boldly,
to venture more seas, where storms shall show your mastery,
where losing sight of land, we shall find the stars.

In the name of the One who pushed back the horizons of our hopes
and invited the brave to follow ... Glory be to the Father ...

---

14 Anthony de Mello, *The Song of the Bird* (Anand, India: Gujarat Sahitja Prakash, 1988), 174-175

God's Melody

'We are God's work of art, created in Christ Jesus' (Ephesians 2:10)

Focusing

Reflection

Rabindranath Tagore writes that the song he wanted to sing has never happened because he has spent his days 'stringing and unstringing' his instrument. Whenever I read these lines a certain sadness enters my soul. I think of how busy my days and nights are, of how I cram my calendar and my life so full at times that my glimpses of God are like a rare and endangered species. I yearn to have the song of God sung in my soul but I, too, keep stringing and unstringing my instrument. I get so preoccupied with the details and pressure of my schedule, with the hurry and worry of life, that I miss the song of goodness which is waiting to be sung through me.

The music of divine love plays uniquely in each person's life. Through individual personalities and personal life events, the goodness of God takes on a melody all its own. The song of God needs an instrument to give it shape and voice. A piano is just a row of keys until someone touches them into life. A violin remains a mute stringed instrument until someone picks it up and touches the strings with song. We are all called to be instruments through which the melody of God takes shape. Through our lives, God's love seeks to dance and make music for the world.[15]

Quiet Prayer

A New Heart

Response: Compassionate God, sing your song in my heart.

Lord, give me a heart that is attuned to the pain in human hearts,
the fear and confusion, the agony and yearning,
give me a heart like yours. *Response.*

Lord, give me a heart that is alive to the yearning in human hearts,
the vision and hope, the desiring and dreaming,
give me a heart like yours. *Response.*

Lord, give me a heart that is open to the newness in human hearts,
the wisdom and prayerfulness, the insight and openness,
give me a heart like yours. *Response.*

Lord, give me a heart that is challenged by the walls in human hearts,
what is choked and closed, what is blocked and stopped,
give me a heart like yours. *Response.*

Lord, give me a heart like yours,
give me your sensitivity when I encounter pain,
your responsiveness when I encounter yearning,
your openness when I encounter what is new,
your tenderness when I encounter what is closed;
Lord, give me a heart like yours. *Response.*

Concluding Prayer

Praised be God who has created us
to sing the music of divine love in the world,
and to give shape to the unspeakable treasure
that is the divine presence in and among us.
May our joyful living out of this knowledge
be to the greater glory of God,
that the song of God's praise may resound to the ends of the earth.

---

15 Joyce Rupp, *May I Have this Dance?* 118

Prayer for People of All Ages

Focusing

Scripture

Abide in me as I abide in you. Just as the branch cannot bear fruit by itself unless it abides in the vine, neither can you unless you abide in me. I am the vine, you are the branches. Those who abide in me and I in them bear much fruit, because apart from me you can do nothing ... My Father is glorified by this, that you bear much fruit and become my disciples. *(John 15:4-5, 8)*

Intercessions for people of all ages

Let us pray for all people of all ages, for all who, young or old, belong to each other and go through life together. Let us pray that we may care for and respect each other, that we may not be divided, but may with one mind try to achieve happiness.

For children

Let us pray for all children, for a happy childhood, and for all among us who are defenceless and small. Let us pray that nothing may harm them; that their lives may not become distorted and perverse; that we do not give them scandal or teach them to hate; but that we may lead them to know the truth; that we may have courage to protect the vulnerable, the immature, the inexperienced among us. *We pray to the Lord; Lord hear our prayer.*

For young people

Let us pray for our young people, whose lives lie ahead of them, that they may go forward with open and receptive minds to meet their future; that they may learn to live with life's uncertainties and face up to disappointments; that they may learn to accept themselves and not lose heart. Let us pray that their wisdom and commitment may be appreciated by older people, so that they may have the scope to change the face of the church and the world. *We pray to the Lord; Lord hear our prayer.*

For adults

Let us pray for those who are in the prime of life, that their lives may be fruitful, that they may not be self-seeking, but seek the welfare of others. We pray for all adults, whether married or single, that they may not be lonely, complacent or closed to others, but that they may go on seeking each others' friendship. Let us pray also for those who cannot find satisfaction and those who have failed, in work or in life, that they may place their hopes in the future and not lose faith in God, our protector who does not want us to be lost. *We pray to the Lord; Lord hear our prayer.*

For old people

Let us pray for all old people, that they may stay young in heart, that they may have wisdom and openness, and not be conservative or envious, but that they may allow latitude to younger people. Let us pray for the aged, that they may not be left behind in life, but still put their experience to good use in the service of others. *We pray to the Lord; Lord hear our prayer.*[16]

Concluding Prayer

Father, protect those you have given to your Son Jesus,
so that your people may be one, as you and Jesus are one.
With your Spirit alive among us, may the world know
that you love your people even as you love Jesus.
May the light of Jesus shine in our lives.
May we love him and keep him among us,
today and every day, world without end.

---

16 Huub Oosterhuis, *Your Word is Near*, 52-55 (adapted)

The World within You

Focusing

> There is a world within you
> no one has ever seen,
> a voice no one has ever heard,
> not even you.
> As yet unknown
> you are your own seer,
> your own interpreter.
> And so, with eyes and ears
> grown sharp, for voice or sign,
> listen well -
> not to these words
> but to that inward voice,
> that impulse beating in your heart
> like a far wave.
> Turn to that source, and you
> will find
> what no one has ever found,
> a ground within you
> no one has ever seen,
> a world beyond the limits
> of your dream's horizon.[17]

Scripture

He looked up and saw rich people putting their gifts into the treasury; he also saw a poor widow put in two small copper coins. He said, 'Truly I tell you, this poor widow has put in more than all of them; for all of them have contributed out of their abundance, but she out of her poverty has put in all she had to live on.' *(Luke 21:1-4)*

Reflection

God has given to each of us the most precious of gifts – more precious even than the great pearl in the field. It is a gift that remains unopened until we reach deep within ourselves and begin to embrace it. As a gift from God it does not hold the same limits as our human understanding. It is, indeed, difficult to image its height and its depth, its length and its breadth. But it is within us, at the very heart of who we are, present from the first moment of the Spirit's breath moving through our being. How sad it would be to reach our final moments and realise that we have never tasted of our gift, that we were too afraid to reach in and accept what God has given us from our first moment of life. How sad it would be to arrive at the end of our journey having never fully lived, having never broken open for the world the treasure within us – the pearl in each of our hearts, the coin of the widow.

Quiet Prayer

Share Reflections/Intercessions

Concluding Prayer

Blessed be the Lord, source of our inward voice,
in whose grace we listen to ourselves,
in whose wisdom we discover what we have to give,
in whose courage we come to dare,
in whose protection we learn to trust,
in whose giving we learn to yield,
in whose living we learn to die,
in whose dying we learn to live.
Glory be ...

---

17 Paul Murray, *The Absent Fountain* (Dublin: Dedalus, 1991), 12

A Cloud of Witnesses

Focusing

Scripture

Now faith is the assurance of things hoped for, the conviction of things not seen. By faith Abel offered to God a sacrifice more acceptable than Cain's. By faith Enoch was taken so that he did not experience death. By faith Noah, warned by God about events as yet unseen, built an ark to save his household. By faith Abraham obeyed when he was called to set out for a place that he was to receive as an inheritance; and he set out, not knowing where he was going.

All of these died in faith without having received the promises, but from a distance saw and greeted them. They confessed that they were strangers and foreigners on the earth, for people who speak in this way make it clear that they are seeking a homeland. Therefore God is not ashamed to be called their God.

By faith Abraham, when put to the test, offered up Isaac. By faith Isaac invoked blessings for the future on Jacob and Esau. By faith Jacob, when dying, blessed each of the sons of Joseph. By faith Joseph, at the end of his life, made mention of the exodus of the Israelites and gave instructions about his burial.

By faith Moses, when he was grown up, refused to be called a son of Pharaoh's daughter, choosing to share ill-treatment with the people of God. By faith he left Egypt, unafraid of the king's anger; for he persevered as though he saw him who is invisible.

By faith the people passed through the Red sea as if it were dry land. By faith the walls of Jericho fell after they had been encircled for seven days. By faith Rahab the prostitute did not perish with those who were disobedient, because she had received the spies in peace.

And what more should I say? For time would fail me to tell of Gideon, Barak, Samson, Jephthah, of David and Samuel and the prophets. Since we are surrounded by so great a cloud of witnesses, let us also lay aside every weight and the sin that clings so closely, and let us run with pereseverance that race that is set before us, looking to Jesus, the pioneer and perfecter of our faith, who for the sake of the joy that was set before him endured the cross, disregarding its shame, and has taken his seat at the right hand of the throne of God. *(from Hebrews 11:1-12:2)*

Quiet Prayer

Shared Reflections/Intercessions

Prayer through our Ancestors
In the trusting faith of Abraham,
we embrace the unknown with confidence.
In the courage and justice of Moses, we set out for the promised land.
In the strength of purpose of Esther,
we give ourselves to what we believe.
In the faithfulness of Ruth, we reach for newness of life.
In the zeal of John of Baptist, we are intoxicated by your coming.
In the wisdom and contemplation of Mary,
we are filled with your presence.
In the adventurous spirit of Paul, we dare to proclaim the good news.

May this cloud of witnesses be to us
as the cloud of your presence to the people in the desert.
May the light of their witness be to us
an encouragement in the struggles of discipleship.
May their faith and hope and love
be our endurance.

A Dream not Dreamt

Focusing

Reflection

> There is a dream
> I have not dreamt
> A vision I have not seen.
> There is in me
> A fearsome longing
> Deep as primordial waters
> And rooted in
> The very womb
> Of earth's fire.
> There is in me
> A life not become,
> Stirring and reaching out
> From the dreams and terrors
> Of dark history.
> There is in me
> A fire not kindled
> Glowing like a lone
> And passionate sentinel
> Awaiting the dawn.
> There is a dream
> I have not dreamt
> A vision
> I have not seen.[18]

Scripture

For surely I know the plans I have for you, says the Lord,
plans for your welfare and not for harm,
to give you a future with hope.
Then when you call on me and come to pray to me,
I will hear you.
When you search for me, you will find me;
if you seek me with all your heart,
I will let you find me, says the Lord.
(Jeremiah 29:11-14)

Quiet Prayer

Shared Reflections/Intercessions

Concluding Prayer

Spirit of Jesus, open our hearts
and give free rein to our dreams.
Let fears be banished and hope be ushered in.
Give us what courage and persistence we need
to make our dreams come true.
Spirit of Jesus,
inspire our imagination with new vision,
and breathe new passion into our lives.
Spirit of Jesus,
may the anticipation of the wonder of the kingdom
be the lifeblood of all our actions.

---

18 Edwina Gateley, *There was no path so I trod one* (Wheathampstead, Herts: Anthony Clarke, 1996), 109

Our Action isn't Everything

*Now to him who by the power at work within us
is able to accomplish abundantly far more than all we can ask or imagine,
to him be glory in the church and in Christ Jesus to all generations,
forever and ever. (Ephesians 3:20-21)*

Focusing

Scripture

But the Lord said to Samuel,
'Do not look on his appearance
or on the height of his stature,
because I have rejected him;
for the Lord does not see as mortals see;
they look on the outward appearance,
but the Lord looks on the heart.'
(1 Samuel 16:7)

Reflection

We live in a world where everything depends on results, on 'delivering'.
But we know from our own work that some of our best efforts seem to
get nowhere. Compared to the energy we invested, the results can
disappoint us deeply. Sometimes it can seem that there is nothing in sight
but disappointment, frustration and confusion.

This make us wonder about the meaning of what we're doing. It jerks
our attention back to what it is that we are doing. It gets us thinking
about the way we think about what we do. Do we really believe that it all
depends on us, that the good we hope to achieve depends simply on our
efforts? Surely the difficulties and disappointments are enough to make
us realise that everything depends, rather, on a power beyond us.

The efforts we put our energy into – we do it all, not because it 'works', but because it is right. We trust in the cause, not in our own efforts or powers. We trust in the power that is working through us, making good in ways that we cannot see beforehand. So we must not trust too much in our own plans. Sometimes they will succeed, oftentimes they will disappoint. We need to trust in the one who continues to work amidst our inevitable disappointments. We need to think of God.

Spirit is always at work, Spirit is always accomplishing. 'Behold, I am with you always!' Let go of your plans, let go of your disappointments. Make room for God. Make room in your eyes for seeing how God works. God works dreams from disappointments, paths in confusion, brightness in bewilderment. Open yourself to God. Your action isn't everything. Yet it can be everything, if you open yourself to God.

Quiet Prayer/Shared Reflections

Concluding Prayer

Lord you are in this place, fill us with your power,
cover us with your peace, show us your presence.
Lord, help us to know we are in your hands,
we are under your protection, we are covered by your love.
Lord, we ask you today to deliver us from evil,
to guide us in our travels, to defend us from all harm.
Lord, give us now eyes to see the invisible, ears to hear your call,
hands to do your work, and hearts to respond to your love.[19]

---

19 David Adam, *Tides and Seasons*, 12

Fill us with your Spirit

Focusing

God, our loving creator and redeemer,
fill our hearts with the life-giving,
joy-giving, peace-giving Spirit of the risen Jesus.
In the power of the Spirit may we praise you now with our lips
and all the day long with our lives.

Scripture

If I look to the mountains,
will they come to my aid?
My help is the Lord,
who made earth and the heavens.

May God, ever wakeful,
keep you from stumbling;
the guardian of Israel
neither rests nor sleeps.

God shields you,
a protector by your side.
The sun shall not harm you by day
nor the moon by night.
(Psalm 121:1-6)

Quiet Prayer

Intercessions

Beloved God, we praise you for the life of your Holy Spirit, inspiring men and women to glorify you in countlessly varied ways. Lord come to bless us with the life of your Spirit.
Bless us Lord with the life of your Spirit.

Beloved God, we bless you for the joy of your Holy Spirit, radiating out into the world from the hope-filled hearts of your disciples. Lord come to bless us with the joy of your Spirit.
Bless us Lord with the joy of your Spirit.

Beloved God, we adore you for the peace of your Holy Spirit, silently yet powerfully turning, easing, comforting, healing human hearts. Lord come to bless us with the peace of your Spirit
Bless us Lord with the peace of your Spirit.

Beloved God, breathe your life-giving, joy-giving, peace-giving Spirit on those to whom we reach out now, to touch with our prayer ...

Quiet, followed by intercessions for those for whom we wish to pray ...

Our Father ...

Concluding Prayer

God our creator and sustainer,
breathe your Spirit upon us,
into our hearts, into our midst, into our work.
May your Spirit inspire all that we do and the way that we do it.
May your Spirit work through each one of us,
to bring harmony among us and joy in our parish community.
Through Christ our Lord.

Called by Name

God most intimate
you are a God close to our hearts.
You have implanted your likeness in us.
You know each of us by name
and constantly send your love
to support us on our way.

Focus

Scripture

You shall be called by a new name that the mouth of the Lord will give.
You shall be a crown of beauty in the hand of the Lord ...
You shall no more be termed Forsaken ...
but you shall be called 'My Delight Is in Her.' *(Isaiah 62:2-4)*

Reflection

Response: O most holy God we praise you, for you have called us by name.

O God, your names are many and most tender:
Gentle One ... Breath Within ... Holy Light ... Gracious Spirit ...
Womb of All ... Keeper of Promises ... Enabling Friend ...
Amazing Grace ... Mystery of Love ... Compassionate Heart ...
Freedom of the Oppressed.
We praise you and your many names
that reveal your constant kindness to all who seek you. *Response.*

God of all seasons and all peoples, we praise you;
throughout time you called women and men by their names
to be prophets, to lead your people, and to be your living presence.
We especially thank you for the liberating name of Jesus.
As your angel called him while he was in Mary's womb,
so is each one of us called and known and loved. *Response.*

Jesus called the disciples by their names and sent them on their mission.
In the name of God and in the name of Jesus
they healed the sick and forgave sins.
As the risen one, Jesus met Mary Magdalene outside the tomb
and called her by name: 'Mary.'
Such is the way that we are called and loved. *Response.*

You reach out to each of us by name and as we are.
As Persistent Friend you call us in the deep recesses of our hearts.
As Intimate One you dine with us.
As Breath of Life you live within us. *Response.*[20]

Quiet Prayer/Intercessions

Concluding Prayer

Lord, as you call each of us by name,
may we call the names of one another
with affection, respect and reverence.
As you accept and love us the way we are,
give us the wisdom and courage to do the same
for ourselves and for all our sisters and brothers.

---

[20] John P. Mossi, *Canticles and Gathering Prayers* (Winona Minnesota, St Mary's Press – Christian
Brothers' Publications, 1989), 117-119 (adapted)

With all creation we praise you, God

Focusing

Reflection

Loving God, all creation calls you blessed.
Your Spirit imprints the whole universe with life and mystery.
Yes, all creation proclaims your love.
We now join with this chorus of praise.

Loving God, all of nature calls you blessed, and so do we.

For you have woven an intimate tapestry and called it life,
and called it good.
From the darkest corners of the cosmos
to the sun-bright droplets of morning dew
you dance the world into being.
Nothing that exists is apart from your love,
no song is sung unheard, no death occurs unmourned.

Loving God, loving God, all creation calls you blessed
and so do we, and so do we.

In love you have formed a universe, so diverse yet so related,
and into its web you call us forth,
to walk the land and swim the sea.
To the stars we seem no more than blades of grass.
Yet to you, each of us, like each blade of grass and each star,
is an irreplacable treasure, an essential companion on this journey of love.

Loving God, loving God, all creation calls you blessed
and so do we, and so do we.

We who are often deaf to your presence
in the many creeds of human hearts
need also to witness your loving presence
in the faith of the forests and the creeds of sky and sea.

And we who are too often silent about your presence
in humans suffering needlessly in our world,
need also to cry out
that the compassion Jesus teaches
goes far beyond our human domain.

*Loving God, loving God, all creation calls you blessed
and so do we, and so do we.*

Loving God, as you lure the whole world into salvation,
guide us with your Spirit
that we might not only be pilgrims on the earth
but pilgrims with the earth, journeying home to you.
Open our hearts to understand your intimacy with all of creation
Only with this faith can we hope that tomorrow's children
will be able to end their prayer as we do now
in Christ's name, world without end. Amen, alleluia!

*Loving God, loving God, all creation calls you blessed
and so do we, and so do we.*[21]

Quiet Prayer

Concluding Prayer

Soak us, creator God, in your Spirit
which flows through tree and cloud and wave,
that we like them would be your praise,
in our every word and gesture,
our every breath and movement.
This we ask through Jesus Christ
whose song of praise you lifted up
to be forever our salvation and your glory.

---

21 John P. Mossi, *Canticles and Gathering Prayers*, 24-26 (adapted)

Fire on Earth

'I came to bring fire to the earth
and how I wish that it were already kindled'
(Luke 12:49)

Reflection

There was a man who invented the art of making fire. He took his tools and went to a tribe in the north, where it was very cold, bitterly cold. He taught the people there to make fire. The people were very interested. He showed them the uses to which they could put fire – they could cook, could keep themselves warm, etc. They were so grateful that they had learned the art of making fire. But before they could express their gratitude to the man, he disappeared. He wasn't concerned with getting their recognition or gratitude; he was concerned about their well-being.

He went to another tribe, where he again began to show them the value of his invention. People were interested there too – a little too interested for the peace of mind of their priests, who began to notice that this man was drawing crowds and they were losing their popularity. So they decided to do away with him. They poisoned him to death. But they were afraid now that the people might turn against them, so they were very wise, even wily.

They had a portrait of the man made, and mounted it on the main altar of the temple. The instruments for making fire were placed in front of the portrait, and the people were taught to revere the portrait and to pay reverence to the instruments of fire. This they dutifully did for centuries. The veneration and worship went on, but there was no fire.[22]

Scripture

As they came near the village to which they were going, he walked ahead as if he were going. But they urged him strongly, saying, 'Stay with us, because it is almost evening and day is now nearly over.' So he went in to stay with them. When he was at the table with them, he took bread, blessed and broke it, and gave it to them. Then their eyes were opened, and they recognised him; and he vanished from their sight. They said to each other, 'Were not our hearts burning within us while he was talking to us on the road, while he was opening the scriptures to us?'
(Luke 24:28-32)

For this reason I remind you to rekindle the gift of God that is within you through the laying on of my hands, for God did not give us a spirit of cowardice, but rather a spirit of power and of love and of self-discipline. *(2 Timothy 1:6-7)*

Quiet Prayer

Shared Reflections/Intercessions

Concluding Prayer

Dear God, beyond us and among us,
set our hearts on fire with the passion of the heart of Jesus.
May we be his passion on earth,
in the particular places where we work,
with the particular people we meet.
Take away our lukewarm hearts;
give us hearts instead ablaze with the desire to see your kingdom come.

---

22 Anthony de Mello, *The Prayer of the Frog*, (Anand, India: Gujarat Sahitja Prakash, 1989), 7 (adapted)

Pilgrim Prayer

Focusing

Reflection

Pilgrim God, there is an exodus going on in my life
– desert stretches, a vast land of questions.
Inside my heart your promises tumble and turn.
No pillar of cloud by day or fire by night that I can see.
My heart hurts at leaving loved ones
and so much of the security I have known.
I try to give in to the stretching and the pain.
It is hard, God, and I want to be settled, secure, safe and sure.
And here I am, feeling so full of a pilgrim's fear and anxiety.

O God of the journey, lift me up, press me against your cheek.
Let your great love hold me and create a deep trust in me.
Then set me down.
God of the journey, take my hand in yours
and guide me ever so gently across the new territory of my life.[23]

Scripture

Know that I am with you and will keep you wherever you go,
and will bring you back to this land;
for I will not leave you until I have done what I have promised you.
(Genesis 28:15)

For surely I know the plans I have for you, says the Lord
plans for your welfare and not for harm,
to give you a future with hope. *(Jeremiah 29:11)*

Quiet Time/Shared Prayer

Prayer

God of my life, create in me the heart of a pilgrim.
There is a part of me that fights letting go.
Do not allow me to become so rooted,
or so accustomed to my daily tasks and inner securities,
that I miss your voice calling me
to greater growth and deeper maturity in faith.

I want to hoard my blessings, to hang onto my gifts,
to hide my talents and the blessings of my life.
I want to take them out only when I know that it is safe
and I won't get hurt or emptied.
Stir afire in me such a great love for you and your people
that I will constantly celebrate life and appreciate its beauty,
even when it is painful.

Allow me to see your visions and dream dreams,
so that I can live with your vision
and not be overwhelmed by the struggles of the journey.
God of the Exodus, I know you are near.
Grant me the courage to change,
whether that change is an inner or an outer one.
Deepen my awareness of your faithful presence,
and bless my pilgrim heart. Amen.[24]

23 Joyce Rupp, *Praying our Goodbyes* (Notre Dame, Indiana: Ave Maria Press, 1988), 125
24 Joyce Rupp, *Praying our Goodbyes*, 126-127

Spirit-Wind

This blast of wind remains invisible, O God,
though I know it in its effects.
The wind makes tall grass sway on a Summer day,
whips a lake into a frenzy,
causes an autumn leaf to jump and swirl.
The wind has such enviable freedom,
going its own way, playing where it pleases ...
Wind of God, blow through my being.

Focusing

Scripture

'The wind blows where it chooses, and you hear the sound of it,
but you do not know where it comes from or where it goes.
So it is with everyone who is born of the Spirit.' *(John 3:8)*

Reflection

We cannot see the Spirit, just as we cannot see the wind. Or can we?
While we cannot see the wind, we can certainly see leaves rustling,
branches swaying, the sea swelling. While we cannot see the wind, we can
certainly hear its roar, its pounding, its whistle. While we cannot see the
wind, we can certainly feel its sharpness on our faces, its iciness on our
ears, its chill in our bones. While we cannot see the wind, we can certainly
smell the odours it brings and taste its flavours, from land and sea and
sky. Of course there are also times so still that we can detect no wind.

We cannot see the Spirit of God, the Spirit of the risen Jesus. But is it because there is no Spirit — just as there is no wind when everything is still? Or is it because we are seeking to see what cannot be seen in itself — anymore than the wind can — rather than seeking its signs? Or again, is it because we ourselves are not doing enough to create such signs, not doing enough to make the Spirit visible and audible and tangible and palpable?

Maybe what we need to do is to make more noise! Maybe there would be more evidence of the Spirit in the world if those in whom the Spirit moves were themselves to make more movement. When the branches sway we 'see' the wind. When God's people proclaim their joy and invest their hope and live their love, then can we 'see' the Spirit. Then there can be no doubt concerning the Spirit.

Quiet Time

Shared Reflections/Prayers

Concluding Prayer

Eternal God of Love,
in you we live and move and have our being.
Breathe through us again this day;
give us the courage to be open
and welcoming to your Spirit
that we may be led to do your will
and follow in your ways,
today and tomorrow. Amen.

The Road of Trust

Beloved Lord
breathe calm in my mind
peace in my heart
and silence in my soul.
In the silence let me hear your voice
in the peace let me see your face
in the calm let me know your love.

Focusing

Scripture

As they came near the village to which they were going, he walked ahead as if he were going. But they urged him strongly, saying, 'Stay with us, because it is almost evening and day is now nearly over.' So he went in to stay with them. When he was at the table with them, he took bread, blessed and broke it, and gave it to them. Then their eyes were opened, and they recognised him; and he vanished from their sight. They said to each other, 'Were not our hearts burning within us while he was talking to us on the road, while he was opening the scriptures to us?'
(Luke 24:28-32)

Reflection

Strangers do not always have to be recognised for us to receive their blessings. But they do need to be trusted. The three strangers who came to Abraham's tent came bearing the good news that Sarah was to have a child. But was it not because the stranger in them was accepted and trusted that they were able to be a blessing in the lives of Sarah and Abraham?

The disciples did not recognise the stranger on the road to Emmaus as Jesus until he broke the bread and vanished from their sight. However, their trusting the stranger that he was must have begun way back on the road when he first started to explain the scriptures to them, and they invited him to stay with them

The stranger you long to recognise as Christ might have to be trusted in some other form, before this deeper recognition can take place.[25]

Quiet Prayer

Shared Reflections/Intercessions

Concluding Prayer

God of all ages, throughout history
you have journeyed with us on our road of discipleship.
In the welcome of Sarah and Abraham,
in the journey of the disciples to Emmaus,
you reveal to us the blessings that are possible for us
when we turn to you in trust and welcome.
Give us the wisdom to look for your presence in the stranger;
grant us the courage to trust in new ways
and lead us to welcome the blessings you send
in the unexpected moments of our lives together.

---

25 Macrina Wiederkehr, *Seasons of your Heart* (San Francisco: Harper, 1991), 162-163

Work

Work

God give me work till my life shall end and life till my work is done.

Meditation

What is this work to which I submit daily?
What is this work that demands my energy, my time, my very self?
What is this work that tells me something of who I am in the world?
What is this work that tells me something of who I choose not to be?

Where is this work that attracts my attention?
Where is this work that calls me to its presence?
Where is this work that beckons both gently and forcibly?
Where is this work that seeks a response?

For whom is this work that warrants my regard?
For whom is this work that draws me into its domain?
With whom is this work that causes me to grapple and despair?
With whom is this work that causes me to rejoice and move forward?

Glory be to God who commissions me as a worker for the Kingdom
Glory be to God whose power working in me is beyond my imagination
Glory be to God whose potential is infinite and incomprehensible
Glory be to God who has called me by name as servant and friend.

Scripture

Who among you would say to your slave,
who has just come in from ploughing or tending sheep in the field,
'Come here at once and take your place at the table'?
Would you not rather say to him,
'Prepare supper for me;
put on your apron and serve me while I eat and drink;
later you may eat and drink.'?
Do you thank the slave for doing what was commanded?
So you also, when you have done all that you were ordered to do, say,
'We are worthless slaves;
we have done only what we ought to have done.'
(Luke 17:7-10)

Quiet Reflection/Shared Prayer

There will be less some day

Creator God,
in the work of our hands, our minds and our spirits
may we constantly reflect the work of the Kingdom.
Grant us the courage
to willingly embrace the mantle of servant,
knowing that as servants of God
we will share in the fruits and joys
of the Kingdom that is and that is to come.
We ask this through the One who came to serve,
Christ our Lord. Amen.

Gospel Blessings

Lord, today brings paths to discover, possibilities to choose,
people to encounter, peace to possess,
promises to fulfil, perplexities to ponder,
power to strengthen, pointers to guide,
pardon to accept, praises to sing
and a Presence to proclaim.[26]

Focusing

Blessings

Blessed are those who realise that they cannot live on bread alone,
but need the word of God too –
they will be fully nourished.

Blessed are those who remember that the things which corrupt us
are not those which enter us but those which come out of us,
and who strive for purity of heart –
they will be clean all over.

Blessed are those who, when they have sinned,
follow the example of the prodigal, and come back home
to seek reconciliation –
they will cause heaven to ring with joy.

Blessed are those who stop to bind up the wounds
of today's roadside wounded,
pouring in the oil of compassion and the wine of hope –
they are the Good Samaritans of today.

Blessed are those generous doers who, in the midst of all their work,
maintain a lonely place in their lives for prayer, reflection and relaxation –
they will not suffer burn-out.

Blessed are those who remove the plank from their own eyes
before telling others to remove the splinter from theirs –
their efforts at reforming others will bear fruit.

Blessed are those who, having put their hand to the plough,
refuse to look back –
they will be found worthy of the kingdom.

Blessed are those disciples who remember that they are the branches
without which the vine cannot bear fruit –
through their good works the Vine will bear the grapes of love.[27]

Quiet Time/

SharedPrayer/Reflections

Concluding Prayer
Creator God,
for the many wonders of our lives we bless your name
and find, in turn, that we are blessed.
Guide and strengthen us on life's journey,
so that we may be the voice and face of Christ in the world,
through our actions, attitudes and presence.
Give us the desire to be instruments of your blessings
in the places of our hearts and homes, both now and tomorrow.
Amen.

---

26 David Adam, *Tides and Seasons*, 42
27 Flor McCarthy, *Windows on the Gospel*, 19

Compassion

The heart of Jesus is a heart of compassion.
In compassion we are most like God.
The Eucharist is the bread of God's compassion for us
and his call for us to be compassionate.

Focusing

Scripture

Be merciful, just as your Father is merciful.
Do not judge, and you will not be judged;
do not condemn, and you will not be condemned.
Forgive and you will be forgiven; give and it will be given to you.
A good measure, pressed down,
shaken together, running over,
will be put into your lap;
for the measure you give
will be the measure you get back.
(Luke 6:36-38)

Meditation

A world in which money and power dominate human and social interaction is a world that is numb. Such a world does not hear the cry of the poor and does not sense the pain of all who suffer. It is the world into which Jesus was born.

As he came to know the world in which he moved, Jesus grew in vision. He imagined a man feeling compassion for another from an enemy community, lying beaten on the side of the road. He imagined a father feeling compassion as he looked upon his wasteful irresponsible son shamefully returning home.

As Jesus' heart was filled with compassion, so too were his deeds. His heart reached out in compassion to the widow of Nain who had lost her only son. As he looked on the crowds who followed him, he felt compassion for them in their lostness and torment and dejection.

In Jesus' heart and hands, the compassion of God penetrates through the numbness of our world. As we break bread in his name, we, who have been touched by his compassion, become his heart and hands in the world.

Quiet Prayer

Be thankful for compassion you have experienced.
Recall compassion you have offered.

Shared Reflections/Prayers

Concluding Prayer

My soul, bless the Lord, bless God's holy name!
My soul, bless the Lord, hold dear all God's gifts!

Bless God, who forgives your sin and heals every illness,
who snatches you from death and enfolds you with tender care,
who fills your life with richness and gives you an eagle's strength.

The Lord is tender and caring, slow to anger, rich in love.
God will not accuse us long, nor bring our sins to trial,
nor exact from us in kind what our sins deserve.

As tender as father to child, so gentle is God to believers.
The Lord knows how we are made, remembers we are dust.
(Psalm 103:1-5, 8-10, 13-14)

Glory be to the Father ...

Giving Thanks

Focusing

Reflection

> O Divine Gift-giver,
> I stand beneath the endless waterfall
> of your abundant gifts to me.
> I thank you especially for the blessing of life,
> the most precious of all your gifts to me.
> I thank you, Ever-generous One,
> for clothing to wear,
> for food and drink to nourish my body,
> for all the talents and skills
> that you have bestowed upon me.
> I thank you for the many joys of my life,
>
> for family and friends,
> for work that gives to me a sense of purpose
> and invests my life with meaning.
> I thank you as well
> for the sufferings and trials of my life
> which are also gifts
> and which together with my mistakes
> are among my most important teachers.
>
> Grant that I may never greet a new day
> without the awareness of some gift
> for which to give you thanks.
> And may constant thanksgiving
> be my song of perpetual praise to you.[28]

Quiet Prayer

Scripture

We always give thanks to God for all of you
and mention you in our prayers,
constantly remembering before our God and Father
your work of faith and labour of love
and steadfastness of hope in our Lord Jesus Christ.
For we know, brothers and sisters beloved by God,
that he has chosen you.
(1 Thessalonians 1:2-4)

Shared Prayer

Conclusion

Let us pray to our benevolent God a litany of thanks
for all the blessings and goodness in our lives.
Response: With heartfelt thanks we bless you O Lord.

For knowing love in our lives,
for the security and confidence and joy it brings;
and for the capacity to love
that we are forever discovering in ourselves...

For the knowledge of you, O God,
whom we discover in so many ways throughout our lives;
and for the passion for your truth
that you have kindled within us...

For the experiences of life,
those that strengthen and those that stretch us,
for in all of them we are learning
to see you working for the good...

Glory be...

---

28 Edward Hays, *Prayers for a Planetary Pilgrim* (Leavenworth KS: Forest of Peace Books, 1989),
197

The Sower

I weave a silence on my lips,
I weave a silence into my mind,
I weave a silence within my heart,
I close my ears to distractions,
I close my eyes to attentions,
I close my heart to temptations.

Calm me, O Lord, as you stilled the storm,
Still me, O Lord, keep me from harm.
Let all the tumult within me cease,
Enfold me, Lord, in your peace.
(Traditional Celtic)

Focusing

Scripture

And he told them many things in parables, saying:
'Listen! A sower went out to sow.
And as he sowed, some seeds fell on the path,
and the birds came and ate them up.
Other seeds fell on rocky ground, where they did not have much soil,
and they sprang up quickly, since they had no depth of soil.
But when the sun rose, they were scorched;
and since they had no root, they withered away.
Other seeds fell among thorns,
and the thorns grew up and choked them.
Other seeds fell on good soil and brought forth grain,
some a hundredfold, some sixty, some thirty.
Let anyone with ears listen!'

Hear then the parable of the sower.
When anyone hears the word of the kingdom
and does not understand it,
the evil one comes and snatches away what is sown in the heart;
this is what was sown on the path.
As for what was sown on rocky ground,
this is the one who hears the word
and immediately receives it with joy;
yet such a person has no root,
but endures only for a while,
and when trouble or persecution arises on account of the word,
that person immediately falls away.
As for what was sown among thorns,
this is the one who hears the word,
but the cares of the world and the lure of wealth
choke the word
and it yields nothing.
But as for what was sown on good soil,
this is the one who hears the word and understands it,
who indeed bears fruit and yields,
in one case a hundredfold,
in another sixty, and in another thirty.
(Matthew 13:3-9, 18-23)

Quiet Prayer

Shared Reflections/Prayers

Concluding Prayer

Gracious God, remove our hearts of stone. Dig away the stoniness of our
hearts. Root out the thorniness in us. Give us hearts of flesh, an open,
receptive soil, ready and eager to embrace your word. May your word
grow in the welcoming soil of our hearts. May it bear fruit for the life of
the world.

Lift up your Hearts

Focusing

> O God, come to our aid.
> O Lord, make haste to help us.
> Glory be to the Father ...

Psalm 121

If I look to the mountains, will they come to my aid?
My help is the Lord, who made earth and the heavens.

May God, ever wakeful, keep you from stumbling;
the guardian of Israel neither rests nor sleeps.

God shields you, a protector by your side.
The sun shall not harm you by day nor the moon at night.

God shelters you from evil, securing your life.
God watches over you near and far, now and always.

Psalm 130

From the depths I call to you, Lord hear my cry.
Catch the sound of my voice raised up, pleading.

If you record our sins, Lord, who could survive?
But because you forgive we stand in awe.

I trust in God's word, I trust in the Lord.
More than sentries for dawn I watch for the Lord.

More than sentries for dawn let Israel watch.
The Lord will bring mercy and grant full pardon.
The Lord will free Israel from all its sins.

Reflection

Blessed be the God and Father of our Lord Jesus Christ!
By his great mercy he has given us a new birth
into a living hope through the resurrection of Jesus Christ from the dead,
and into an inheritance that is imperishable,
undefiled, and unfading, kept in heaven for you.
Although you have not seen him you love him;
and even though you do not see him now,
you believe in him and rejoice with an indescribable and glorious joy.
(1 Peter 1:3-4, 8)

Intercessions

Concluding Prayer

Lifting our hearts and prayers to you, O God,
we remember that in days of old
you gave a new heart to the people of Israel.
O God, give to us a renewed heart.

You gave a new heart to the disciples
as they followed in the ways of Christ.
O God, give to us a renewed heart.

You gave a new heart to the martyrs
as they stood upright and endured for the love of the gospel.
O God, give to us a renewed heart.

Ever faithful to the promises you made,
you continue to give new heart to your people.
O God, give to us a renewed heart.

God of newness, renew our hearts;
heart of God, make us new.

Fathering and Mothering God

Focusing

Reflection

> *God our Father, your will be done, on earth as in heaven.*
> *We thank you for giving us the bread we need. Holy is your name.*

You hold us in your strong arms like a mother with her new-born infant. You have raised your children from generation to generation, planting seeds, harvesting grain, baking fresh bread, preparing meals, feeding your people, holding us up when we are too weak to stand on our own, teaching us how to walk and enabling us to go forth in the world as your daughters and sons.

> *God our Mother, you are the womb of our power, our tenderness and our courage. We forget too often that you are God. Holy is your name.*

We who are as varied as your names are numerous, as varied as the ways in which you reveal yourself to us, we delight to be your cooperative, imaginative workers in a world abundant with redemptive images.

> *God our Father, your will be done, on earth as in heaven.*
> *We thank you for giving us the bread we need. Holy is your name.*

We see you in the sun and the moon, the rain and the wind, coming with power. We see you in the liberation of humanity from injustice and oppression. We see you coming with power. Holy is your name.

> *God our Mother, you are the womb of our power, our tenderness and our courage. We forget too often that you are God. Holy is your name.*

We see you in our friends and lovers, our spouses and children. We know your passion, your commitment to right relations amongst us. We experience you, coming with power.

God our Father, your will be done, on earth as in heaven.
We thank you for giving us the bread we need. Holy is your name.

We see you in the bodies of hungry people, broken people, tortured people, and in a tortured earth. We tremble, yet we believe that you are coming with power. Holy is your name.

God our Mother, you are the womb of our power, our tenderness and our courage. We forget too often that you are God. Holy is your name.

We believe in you, we love you, we expect you to be with us, as we remember the power you revealed to us in the life of Jesus, your Son and our brother. Amen.
(Eucharistic Prayer, Center of Concern)

Quiet Prayer

Shared Reflections/Prayers

Concluding Prayer

Come, Lord, with power into our midst.
Come with power into our prayer.
Come with power into our lives.
Come with power into our work.
Come with power into our togetherness.
Transform our prayer, our lives, our work, our togetherness,
that we may more truly be the body of Christ,
your beloved and our Saviour. Amen.

Longing for the Lord

The arms of God reach round us,
we rest in their embrace;
the heart of Jesus invites us,
we look upon his face;
the Spirit breathes upon us,
welcome, this time of grace.

Focusing

A Psalm of Longing

My spirit hungers for your love, O divine Maker of hearts
for the taste of your joy and the aroma of your peace.
May this time of prayer fill me with the whisper of your presence
and let me feel the touch of your hand upon my heart.
How I long for the depths of your love, to know your quiet constancy,
the feast of your friendship that feeds me without end.
Oh, how my soul longs for you.
You elude all the names we give you
and dwell beyond the grasp of brilliant minds.
Your essence pulses within every atom
yet extends beyond the far frontiers of space,
unscanned by the strongest telescopes.
Awaken me to your presence, now, this moment, in my heart.[29]

Scripture

Now the boy Samuel was ministering to the Lord under Eli. The word of
the Lord was rare in those days; visions were not widespread. At that
time Eli, whose eyesight had begun to grow dim so that he could not see,
was lying down in his room; the lamp of God had not yet gone out and
Samuel was lying down in the temple of the Lord, where the ark of God
was. Then the Lord called, 'Samuel! Samuel!' and he said, 'Here I am!'
and ran to Eli, and said, 'Here I am, for you called me.' But he said, 'I

did not call; lie down again.' So he went and lay down. The Lord called again, 'Samuel!' Samuel got up and went to Eli, and said, 'Here I am, for you called me.' But he said, 'I did not call, my son; lie down again.'

Now Samuel did not yet know the Lord, and the word of the Lord had not yet been revealed to him. The Lord called Samuel again, a third time. And he got up and went to Eli, and said, 'Here I am, for you called me.' Then Eli perceived that the Lord was calling the boy. Therefore Eli said to Samuel, 'Go, lie down; and if he calls you, you shall say, "Speak Lord, for your servant is listening."' So Samuel went and lay down in his place. Now the Lord came and stood there, calling as before, 'Samuel! Samuel!' And Samuel said, 'Speak, for your servant is listening.' Then the Lord said to Samuel, 'See, I am about to do something in Israel that will make both ears of anyone who hears of it tingle.' *(1 Samuel 3:1-11)*

Quiet Time

Shared Reflections/Intercessions

Blessing
The blessing of the God who created us,
the blessing of the Son who is our redemption,
the blessing of the Spirit living within us
come upon us now to guide and protect us. Amen.

---

29 Edward Hays, *Prayers for a Planetary Pilgrim*, 172

Prayer of the Compulsive Worker

Let your loveliness shine on us,
and bless the work we do,
bless the work of our hands.
(Psalm 90:17)

Focusing

Scripture

If the Lord does not build the house, the builders work in vain.
If the Lord does not watch over the city, the guards watch in vain.
How foolish to rise early and slave until night for bread.
Those who please God receive as much even while they sleep.
(Psalm 127:1-2)

Reflection

Christian tradition is full of the idea that everything depends on God.
Paul says to the Corinthians, "I planted, Apollos watered, but God gave
the growth." St Ignatius tells us to act as if everything depended on us
and to await the results as if everything depended on God. Today we hear
it said that in doing the work of the Lord we should not forget the Lord
of the work.

But Christian tradition is also full of people making the mistake of thinking that it all depends on themselves, that the work of the builders is
what matters. Many have become enslaved by their work. We think it has
to be done this week, or today. We think it has to be done by us, that we
are indispensable.

In becoming enslaved and addicted to work, people are becoming
alienated from themselves. They are losing sight of what life is all about.

They are forgetting about relationships. They are ceasing to wonder, to contemplate, losing their inner silence. Days, weeks, months pass by in a frantic haze of work, but it is life that is slipping away.

Lord, protect and preserve us from the addiction and alienation of work and from the illusion of being indispensable. Let us not lose sight of ourselves and of what really matters. Let us approach our work with light hearts and with humble hearts. Bless us with inner peace and ease the tension in our lives. Let us know the passion and the detachment of life lived in your presence and for your name.

Quiet Time

Shared Prayers

Concluding Prayer

We pray to you, Lord, for the gift and grace of balance.
May our lives be blessed with gracious, harmonious balance.
May we invest ourselves in our work,
yet not forget that it is you who is working through us.
May we invest ourselves in activity,
yet not neglect the precious prayer and reflection
that gives our activity depth.
May we invest ourselves in our tasks,
yet not lack appreciation for the relationships close to our hearts.
Grant that we may be both serious and happy,
both hard-working and relaxed,
both passionate and at peace. Amen.

A Disciple's Path

Focusing

> *Let us pause to give thanks to God for all those who minister to us in the church and who serve us in our daily lives … (pause) … In this awareness and appreciation of how we are ministered to, let us pray about our own calling to ministry and service.*

Scripture

There are varieties of gifts, but the same Spirit; and there are varieties of services, but the same Lord; and there are varieties of activities, but it is the same God who activates all of them in everyone. To each is given the manifestation of the Spirit for the common good. *(1 Corinthians 12:4-7)*

Reflection

Show me, Lord, the disciple's path

In you, O Lord, I live and move and have my being;
in you I place my trust.
Do not let me be put to shame,
or be ridiculed by those who have chosen other ways.
No one who follows you need feel ashamed,
only those who are unfaithful for no reason.

Show me, Lord, the disciple's path, teach me your ways.
Give me the courage to walk in your footsteps
for they lead to salvation.
Remember your goodness and faithful love, shown throughout the ages.

Recall not the sins of my youth
but in your goodness remember me in love.
For you are just and upright, generous and kind,
to those faithful to your covenant.
You guide the humble and teach those in need,
You lovingly guide your people in your ways.

Lord, my eyes are set on you,
for only you will free me from the dangers of life,
In my times of loneliness and despair turn to me and lift me up.
Relieve the troubles of my heart
and bring me out of what binds me in life.
When I have been wounded by my own sin
reach out to me with healing and forgiveness.

Lord, in you I place my trust, as your disciple I turn to you.
In the path ahead you are my light, my protection.
For in each step I take, all my hope is in you.
(Based on psalm 25)

Quiet Prayer

Shared Reflections/Intercessions

Concluding Prayer

Gracious God, we know that the heart of your being
is a passionate concern for all your creation and all your creatures.
We bless you for the life of Jesus of Nazareth
and for the Spirit of his living presence among us,
inspiring in our hearts a murmur of your passion.
We bless you for calling us in this way to be your disciples,
for seeing in each of us the possibility and the potential
to be your heart and passion for the world.
May we listen attentively to your movement within us;
may grow more alert to where your call is leading us;
and thus be true and faithful disciples. Amen.

Struggle and Contemplation

We need no wings to go in search of him,
but have only to find a place where we can be alone
and look upon him present within us.
(Teresa of Avila)

Focusing

Reflection

There is a Life hidden in us, a Life which rouses our hope.
It opens a way forward, the way of a becoming for each person
and for all humanity.
Will you focus your attention on it?
Without this hope, anchored at the very heart of your heart,
without this becoming stretched out beyond yourself,
you lose any desire to forge ahead.
No sheer projection of your own wishes,
but a hope which leads you to live in ways
which seemed to lie beyond all hope,
even in situations with no issue ...

When you let your world revolve around yourself,
you are plunged into self-centredness,
all your powers of creation and love dislocated.
To displace this centre, and for love to be kindled there,
you are offered the same fire offered to every person in the world –
his Spirit in you.
His impetus, his spontaneity, his inspiration
have only to waken, for life to become intense and real.

In the vanguard of the church, will you be a carrier of living waters?
Will you quench the thirst of all who are searching for the source?
Peace and justice are not served merely by the desire for them.

It is still essential to go to the source
and reconcile in oneself struggle and contemplation ...

In prayer and in the search for justice,
saying without doing would make you one of the oppressors.
Never let yourself be trapped in the alternative,
either commitment to the oppressed or the quest for sources.
Not struggle or contemplation, but both together,
one springing from the other.

This radicalism of the gospel demands too much
for you to pass judgment on those who do not understand.
Even if you are not understood, do not stand still.
You are the one to take this risk.
A hand to grasp your own, to lead you out along the way.
No one can do that for another ...
Only he who has recognised you already.[30]

Quiet Prayer

Shared Reflections/Prayers

Prayer of Columba
Be thou a bright flame before me,
be thou a guiding star above me,
be thou a smooth path below me,
be thou a kindly shepherd behind me
today – tonight – and forever.

---

30 Brother Roger of Taizé, *A Life We Never Dared Hope For* (Oxford: Mowbray, 1980), 8-9

The Seasons of Life

God of our beginning and our end
God of all the times in our life
God in despondency, God in ecstasy
God in light and in darkness too
God who exhilirates, God who disappears
God in success and in failure too;
God you are our all, to you we turn;
Engender in our hearts this day
A peace-filled silence as we pray.

Focusing

Scripture

For everything there is a season, and a time for every matter under heaven;
a time to be born, and a time to die;
a time to plant, and a time pluck up what is planted;
a time to kill, and a time to heal;
a time to break down, and a time to build up;
a time to weep, and a time to laugh;
a time to mourn, and a time to dance;
a time to throw away stones, and a time to gather stones together;
a time to embrace, and a time to refrain from embracing;
a time to seek, and a time to lose;
a time to keep, and a time to throw away;
a time to tear, and a time to sew;
a time to keep silence, and a time to speak;
a time to love, and a time to hate;
a time for war, and a time for peace.
(Ecclesiastes 3:1-8)

Quiet Prayer

Meditating quietly on how the 'times' of Ecclesiastes are reflected and expressed in the lives of God's people, for instance, some of the following:
- *Teenage sons and daughters*
- *People growing old*
- *Family growing up, children moving on*
- *Men and women in the middle of life*
- *Little children*
- *People on their own*
- *People searching and thirsting*
- *Those on the fringes*
- *People in unusual situations*
- *Unrecognised people*
- *People carrying burdens*
- *Those exercising leadership*
- *People who've been hurt*
- *Married couples*
- *Those out in the cold*
- *People with hidden gifts*
- *Ones who lack confidence*
- *Those who are dying*
- *Those who are being born*
- *(Other)*

Shared Reflections

Concluding Prayer

Wilt thou not yield us vision, God of grace,
of that vast realm, that unhorizoned space
which is thy heart,
and heart-room makes for all.
(Old Celtic prayer)

Embracing the Lord's Call

Focusing

Scripture

You are my friends if you do what I command you. I do not call you servants any longer, because the servant does not know what the master is doing; but I have called you friends, because I have made known to you everything I have heard from my Father. You did not choose me, but I chose you. And I appointed you to go and bear fruit, fruit that will last, so that the Father will give you whatever you ask him in my name. *(John 15:14-16)*

Call Waiting / Call Answering

We spend so much time in life waiting to be called ... waiting to be called for a job interview ... waiting to be called by a friend to invite us out ... waiting to be called from a queue ... waiting to be called for our dinner ... waiting to be called out of bed by an alarm clock ... waiting to be called for a medical appointment ...

But God has already called us. There is no waiting time, just answering time, responding time. All our life is caught up in responding to this call by God. All our life is about bringing this call to fruition in the time with which we have been gifted.

So do we continue to wait for a call that has already been given or do we embrace it today and enter into the life to which it leads us? Do we wait and say not yet, Lord, I am not ready, or do we acknowledge that God has given us everything we need to make the call a reality? Do we listen to the call within our hearts and thereby enter deeper into our lives? Do we dare to dream in partnership with God and help bring the gospel vision to today's world?

Quiet Prayer

Praying through our ancestors

Let us pray, mindful of those who have gone before us, our ancestors. In their witness may we be helped to respond to God's call ...

Adam and Eve, the first humans God called into being. In their failure we recognise our own humanity; in their separation from God we feel our own alienation. To Adam and Eve through Christ our Lord we say:
Pray for us.

Abraham, our father in faith, called to trust in God even in the darkest moment. In our own lives we are called into moments of darkness. To Abraham through Christ our Lord we say:
Help us to trust.

Sarah, wife of Abraham and mother of Isaac, called to wait patiently for the gift of motherhood. In our lives we too are called to wait for new beginnings. To Sarah through Christ our Lord we say:
Fill our patient and waiting hearts.

Moses, reluctant leader of God's people, called to new and challenging ways. In God's call to us we sometimes only feel the fear. To Moses through Christ our Lord we say:
Give us your courage to approach the burning bush before us.

Ruth and Naomi, called to loyalty and care. In the choices they faced we recognise the choices we are called to make in our lives. To Ruth and Naomi through Christ our Lord we say:
Help us to embrace loyalty and choose the way of our call.

Mary, mother of Jesus, our mother too. Called to a life of deep trust, she pondered in her heart the call of God, as we too are urged to ponder it. To Mary we say:
Give us burning hearts to respond to God's call.

All: Our Father ...

Carers Need Caring

Focusing

Reflection

More than anything, I have learned that we are all frail people,
vulnerable and wounded;
it is just that some of us conceal it more than others!
But the truth is that it is alright to be frail and wounded,
because that is the way the almighty, transcendent God finds us
and accepts us.

The world is not divided into the strong who care
and the weak who are cared for.
We must each in turn care and be cared for –
not just because it is good for us,
but because that it the way things are.
The hardest thing for those of us who are 'fulltime' carers
is to admit that we are in need,
to peel off our sweaty socks
and let someone else wash our blistered feet.

And when at last we have given in
and have allowed someone to care for us,
perhaps there is a certain inertia
which makes us want to cling to the role of patient,
reluctant to take up the task of serving once more.
It is easy to forget that so much caring, so much serving
is done by people who are weary and in some way not quite whole.
Because we want our carers to be strong and invulnerable,
we project on to them qualities which they do not have.

But again, perhaps that is the way things are,
because that is the way people are,
and we must learn to be strong for those who need us most urgently
and relax and lower our guard
with those who will accept our weakness and cherish us.

Scripture

Six days before the Passover Jesus came to Bethany,
the home of Lazarus, whom he had raised from the dead.
There they gave a dinner for him.
Martha served, and Lazarus was one of those at the table with him.
Mary took a pound of costly perfume made of pure nard,
anointed Jesus' feet, and wiped them with her hair.
The house was filled with the fragrance of the perfume.
(John 12:1-3)

Quiet Time

Shared Prayers/Reflections

Concluding Prayer

We are told that it is more blessed to give than to receive.
We give thanks to the Lord for the insight
that in giving we discover our deepest selves.
Now we thank the Lord for the sister insight,
that in giving we must also learn to receive.
We pray for intuition and courage
to acknowledge our need of what others give.
We pray for the generosity to give to others
the possibility of giving to us. Amen.

The Yeast of Hope

Focusing

Scripture

The kingdom of heaven
is like yeast that a woman took
and mixed in with three measures of flour
until all of it was leavened.
(Matthew 13:33)

Meditation

Christians are meant to be a leaven for our society. We are called to rise
in all directions with the healing presence of our lives. Part of the noble
task of our vocation is to help people discover the hint of eternity that
flows through the inner rivers of their beings. This hint of eternity will
nurture their hope. Hope is contagious. Hope is like yeast and baking
powder. It has the energy that makes things rise. If you want to know if
you are good for others, ask yourself how much hope you've given them.
It is there you will find your answer.

> *I was just thinking*
> *one morning*
> *during meditation*
> *how much alike*
> *hope*
> *and baking powder are:*
> *quietly*
> *getting what is*
> *best in me*
> *to rise,*
> *awakening*

the hint of eternity
within.
I always think of that
when I eat biscuits now
and wish
that I could be
more faithful
to the hint of eternity.
the baking powder
in me.[31]

Quiet Prayer/Shared Prayer

Let Nothing Disturb You

Response: For God is unchanging, God is ever true; God who loves you so.

Let nothing disturb you or take away your peace,
make your home in God.
Let nothing alarm you or hold your heart in fear.
Know that all things fade away.

So be patient with what is and everything is yours,
all you need your God will give.
For with God in your heart and your faith strong in him
know that you will forever live.

Let nothing disturb you or take away your peace.
Make your home, make your home, make your home in God.
(Teresa of Avila)

---

31 Macrina Wiederkehr, *Seasons of your Heart,* 56-57

God in the Stillness

Focusing

Mobile phones ... answering machines ... voice mail ...
fax machines ... e mails ... internet ...
So much communication, so many messages, so many voices ...
Which are true? Which are important?
With such a flurry of communication, such a rush of messages,
do we remember how to listen?
Perhaps the most important messages come in very quiet ways ...

Scripture

Elijah went a day's journey into the wilderness, and came and sat down under a solitary broom tree. He asked that he might die: 'It is enough; now, O Lord, take away my life, for I am no better than my ancestors.' Then he lay down under the broom tree and fell asleep. Suddenly an angel touched him and said to him, 'Get up and eat.' He looked, and there at his head was a cake baked on hot stones, and a jar of water. He ate and drank, and lay down again. The angel of the Lord came a second time, touched him, and said, 'Get up and eat, otherwise the journey will be too much for you.' He got up, and ate and drank; then he went in the strength of that food forty days and forty nights to Horeb the mount of God. At that place he came to a cave, and spent the night there.

Then the word of the Lord came to him, saying ... 'Go out and stand on the mountain before the Lord, for the Lord is about to pass by.' Now there was a great wind, so strong that it was splitting mountains and breaking rocks to pieces before the Lord, but the Lord was not in the wind; and after the wind an earthquake, but the Lord was not in the earthquake; and after the earthquake a fire, but the Lord was not in the fire; and after the fire, a sound of sheer silence. When Elijah heard it, he wrapped his face in his mantle and went out and stood at the entrance of the cave ... *(1 Kings 19:4-9, 11-13)*

Quiet Prayer

Intercessions
Response: Calm us, Lord, and fill us with your presence.

Lord, teach us to live life at a human pace – not a snail's pace and not a frantic pace, but a pace that gives us space and allows us to attend to what is really going on.

Lord, give us the gift of quiet at those times when our hearts are at their most restless and our lives at their most disjointed and our work at its most chaotic. May pressure never tempt us to postpone your quiet coming.

Lord, bless us with the peace of heart that is able to resist the grip of tasks and goals and projects, so as to be always available to our sisters and brothers. May we be responsive to the needs and the pain of others.

Lord, help us to listen well to your call within and about us. As we invest ourselves in the detail of our work, let us always keep vividly before us the mission you have given us. May the passion for your kingdom never abate within us.

Concluding Prayer
God of the listening heart,
God of quiet, ever attentive to the cries of your people,
ever compassionate in our pain,
bless us with the peace of your divine heart.
We ask this through Christ our Lord. Amen.

Paths

I weave into my life this day
The Presence of God upon my way,
I weave into my life this hour
The mighty God and all his power.
I weave into my sore distress
His peace and calm and no less.
I weave into my step so lame
Heaving and helping of His name.
I weave into the darkest night
Strands of God shining bright,
I weave into each deed done
Joy and hope of the Risen Son.[32]

Focusing

Reflections

Now I yearn for one of those old, meandering, dry, uninhabited roads which lead away from towns ... where you may forget in what country you are travelling ... along which you may travel like a pilgrim, going nowhither; where travellers are not too often to be met; where my spirit is free; where the walls and fences are not cared for; where your head is more in heaven than your feet are on earth ... *(H.D. Thoreau)*

Afoot and light-hearted I take to the open road,
Healthy, free, the world before me,
The long brown path before me leading wherever I choose.
Henceforth I ask not good fortune – I myself am good fortune;
Henceforth I whimper no more, postpone no more, need nothing,
Done with indoor complaints, libraries, querulous criticisms,
Strong and content I travel the open road.
(Walt Whitman, Song of the Open Road)

Quiet Prayer

Scripture

Teach me how to live, Lord, show me the way.
Steer me toward your truth, you, my saving God,
you, my constant hope.

Recall your tenderness, your lasting love.
Remember me, not my faults, the sins of my youth.
To show your own goodness, God, remember me.

Good and just is the Lord, guiding those who stray.
God leads the poor, pointing out the path.

God's ways are faithful love for those who keep the covenant.
(Psalm 25:4-10)

Intercessions

Closing Prayer

O God, I know that all of life,
each path, is a path of promise if travelled in you.
As we seek to root our lives in you,
may we learn to trust the path we travel.
May we put our trust in your leading us
rather than in our own interests.
Bless us with the strength to follow wherever your will leads us.
Through Christ our Lord, Amen.

---

32 David Adam, *Tides and Seasons,* 120

Believing in the New

And the one who was seated on the throne said,
'See, I am making all things new.'
(Revelation 21:5)

Focusing

Scripture

Thus says the Lord, who makes a way in the sea, a path in the mighty
waters, who brings out chariot and horse, army and warrior; they lie
down, they cannot rise, they are extinguished, quenched like a wick; Do
not remember the former things, or consider the things of old. I am
about to do a new thing; now it springs forth, do you not perceive it? I
will make a way in the wilderness and rivers in the desert.
(Isaiah 43:16-19)

Reflection

To be a Christian is to have received new life, to have become new life.
'The old has passed away; behold the new has come!' Through baptism,
our old selves have been buried in the tomb of Christ and we have risen
with him to newness of life. Surely one of the most amazing and
provocative thoughts in our faith! Yet how little the impact it makes on us.

Indeed, how often do the lives we live contradict the truth of what we
are! We stay stuck in the tomb, we cling to what is dying, we lack faith in
what is being born. We fear the light of the dawning sun. Sometimes we
do not notice even, so accustomed have we become to what is familiar
and comfortable.

To be a Christian is to believe in the new. To be a Christian is to believe
in a God of newness, perpetually active among us, forever bringing the
new out of the old, transforming the tomb of death into a womb of new
life. To be a Christian is to dare to attempt to see as God sees

Quiet Reflection

Sharing of Prayers/Reflections

Litany of Hope
We believe in God
the one who reveals new life when all seems dead.
We believe in the New
in the incarnation, which renews the face of the earth.
We believe in Christ
the pledge to us of God's promise of new life.
We believe in the New
in the possibilities in our midst that challenge us to see with new eyes.
We believe in the Spirit
whose power within enables us to make things new.
We believe in the New
the new heaven and earth coming to birth before our eyes.

Concluding Prayer
Christ now sits at the right hand of the Father
and calls us into God's future.
His going ahead of us assures us about what is new.
May the Lord who lies ahead of us and beckons us forward
teach us to trust the unknown and to embrace new life,
now and every day. Amen.

All our Tomorrows

If I could wish for something
I would wish for neither wealth nor power but the passion for possibility.
I would wish only for an eye which, eternally young,
eternally burns with the longing to see possibility.
(Kierkegaard)

Focusing

Scripture

For truly I tell you, if you have faith the size of a mustard seed, you will say to this mountain, 'Move from here to there,' and it will move; and nothing will be impossible for you. *(Matthew 17:20-21)*

Reflection

I can remember being told to reach for the stars. Maybe not in so many words, but as part of the stories I was told as a child, and the dreaming they inspired. And as part of my passage into the adult world, in the confident young sense that I could make a difference, perhaps even change the world.

And then I can remember being told not to be idealistic, not to be a dreamer. 'That's very idealistic.' 'That's all very well in theory.' 'It's a lovely idea but ...' I learned that to be idealistic was to be unreal. And so I learned to be practical. To think in terms of what is manageable, what is possible.

Then I recall hearing the phrase, 'aim for the stars and you'll hit the sky; aim for the sky and you'll hit the ceiling'. For a while it seemed to reconcile in me being an idealist and being a realist. Until I realised that it turns away from the possibility of reaching the stars.

Now I find myself asking myself, 'what is my Lord calling for from me – to be an idealist or to be a realist?' Something tells me that the answer is both. But another voice speaks to me about the resurrection of our bodies, about the coming of the kingdom of God, about the fulness of the body of Christ, about a new heaven and a new earth. And I wonder. Perhaps being idealistic is to see the world in a very positive way. Perhaps being realistic can mean the opposite.

Quiet Prayer

Intercessions

Response: For all that has been, thanks; for all that shall be, yes.

Lord of time, God of eternity, bring healing to our past,
mistakes made, harm done, opportunites squandered,
reconciliation not sought for.
May the risen Christ bring peace to our memory.

Lord of time, God of eternity, teach us vigilance in the present,
that we may seek out, be alive and responsive
to what your Spirit is saying to us, to the hope hidden in everything.

Lord of time, God of eternity, enlighten the future for us;
strengthen our resolve, revitalise our vision,
ensure our perseverance, enhance our hope.

God of past, present and future,
we remember in joy all that you have done for us in Jesus of Nazareth.
We look forward in anticipation
to the completion of your work of salvation.
We give ourselves in willing commitment to the work of your Spirit
in our place on earth.

Glory be to the Father, the Son and the Holy Spirit.
As it was in the beginning, is now, and ever shall be,
world without end. Amen.

Hands

Focusing

Scripture

I will not forget you. See, I have inscribed you on the palms of my hands. *(Isaiah 49:15-16)*

Then the Lord put out his hand and touched my mouth; and the Lord said to me, 'Now I have put my words in your mouth.' *(Jeremiah 1:9)*

Just like the clay in the potter's hand, so are you in my hand, O house of Israel. *(Jeremiah 18:6)*

While they were eating, Jesus took a loaf of bread, and after blessing it he broke it, gave it to the disciples ... *(Matthew 26:26)*

Then they spat in his face and struck him; and some slapped him ... *(Matthew 26:67)*

A leper came to him begging him, and kneeling he said to him, 'If you choose, you can make me clean.' Moved with pity, Jesus stretched out his hand and touched him, and said to him, 'I do choose. Be made clean!' *(Mark 1:40-41)*

'Let anyone among you who is without sin be the first to throw a stone at her.' *(John 8:7)*

Then he poured water into a basin and began to wash the disciples' feet and to wipe them with the towel that was tied around him. *(John 13:5)*

Meditation

Let us ponder awhile the images of these scripture passages ... and what they reveal about the power and potential of our hands ... with our hands we can create ... nurture ... cradle ... heal ... serve ... caress ... soothe ...beckon ... liberate ... share ... hold ... let go ... release ... forgive ... empower.

But with these hands we can also destroy ... beat down ... cast aside ... condemn ... tear apart ... wound ... imprison ... deny ... reject ... belittle.

Through all these actions of our hands we reveal some truth of our inner selves to the world. The intimacy of our touch echoes the intimacy of our hearts ...

As followers of Christ, how will we choose to share his gentle touch with the world? What work will we give our hands this day? And how will that work share in partnership with the work of Christ?

Quiet Time/Shared Prayer

Concluding Prayer

For the gift of our hands and the power of their touch
We bless you God, our creator.
For the wonderful example of your healing touch
We bless you Jesus, our redeemer.
For the grace that leads us to reach out
and transform the world through our being
We bless you, life-giving Spirit.

We pray, in the name of the beloved Trinity,
that all the work and gestures of our hands
will contribute to the building of your kingdom among us.
We ask this through Christ our Lord.

Fruitful Lives in God

Focusing

Meditation

The fruit of silence is prayer
The fruit of prayer is faith
The fruit of faith is love
The fruit of love is service
The fruit of service is peace.
(Mother Teresa)

Scripture

Beware of false prophets, who come to you in sheep's clothing
but inwardly are ravenous wolves.
You will know tham by their fruits.
Are grapes gathered from thorns, or figs from thistles?
In the same way, every good tree bears good fruit,
but the bad tree bears bad fruit.
A good tree cannot bear bad fruit,
nor can a bad tree bear good fruit.
Every tree that does not bear good fruit
is cut down and thrown into the fire.
Thus you will know them by their fruits.

Not everyone who says to me, 'Lord, Lord,'
will enter the kingdom of heaven,
but only the one who does the will of my Father in heaven.
(Matthew 7:15-21)

Closing Prayer RCIA
11/10/99

(Christian Service —
the ACTIVE CATHOLIC —
Jane's presentation)
FRUITFUL LIVES IN GOD

Quiet Prayer/Shared Prayer

God Counts on Us

Only God creates
    but we are called to enhance that creation.
Only God gives life
    but we are called to cherish life.
Only God makes to grow
    but we are called to nourish that growth.
Only God gives faith
    but we are called to be signs of God for each other.
Only God gives love
    but we are called to care for each other.
Only God gives hope
    but we are called to give each other reason to hope.
Only God gives power
    but we are called to get things going.
Only God can bring peace
    but we are called to build bridges.
Only God brings happiness
    but we are invited to be joyful.
Only God is the way
    but we are called to show the way to others.
Only God is light
    but we are called to make that light shine in the world.
Only God makes miracles happen
    but we must offer our loaves and fishes.
Only God can do the impossible
    but it's up to us to do what *is* possible.

Our Father ...

Dream God's Dream

Focusing

Meditation

And the Lord God said
I myself will dream a dream with you
Good dreams come from me, you know
My dreams seem impossible
Not too practical
Not for the cautious man or woman
A little risky sometimes
A trifly brash perhaps
Some of my friends prefer to rest more comfortably
In sounder sleep
With visionless eyes
But from those who share my dreams
I ask a little patience
A little humour
Some small courage
And a listening heart
I will do the rest
Then they will risk
And wonder at their daring
Run and marvel at their speed
Build and stand in awe at the beauty of their building
You will meet me often as you work
In your companions who share your risk
In your friends, who believe in you enough
To lend their own dreams
Their own hands
Their own hearts
To your building

In the people who will find your doorway
Stay awhile, and walk away
Knowing they too can find a dream
There will be sun-filled days
And sometimes it will rain
A little variety!
Both come from me
So come now
Be content
It is my dream you dream
My house you build
My caring you witness
My love you share

Quiet Prayer

Shared Reflections/Intercessions

Concluding Prayer

O God who created us,
fill our minds with knowledge and appreciation of the dream
with which and for which you created us.
O God who created us,
fill our hearts with courage to take the risks
and pay the price that will make this dream come true.
O God who created us, breathe life and energy into our hands,
and we will always find joy in dreaming your dream into reality.
Through Christ our Lord. Amen.

Sacrament of Silence

Focusing

Meditation

Silence is sound from the future, an intimation of eternity. Eternity has begun for me. I carry eternity within me; it is slowly, silently growing out of me. More is becoming eternalised, forevered. 'Whoever really possesses the Word of Jesus can sense also his silence' (Ignatius of Antioch). Silence is our way of going into the desert, into eternity.

We each carry our own depth of silence, the human kind of silence not found anywhere else … Silence is a presence, a receptivity, a readiness, a waiting, a listening. There are different kinds of silence, expressing contentment, fulness, or emptiness. Silence has many different faces, meanings. There is the silence of wisdom and the silence of ignorance, the silence of humility and the silence of poverty, the silence of anger and the silence of love. There is the silence of Jesus among us for thirty years, the silence of Nazareth, of Bethlehem, of the desert, of the nights on the mountain.

There is the silence of nature, the turning of the earth, its movement around the sun, the silence of the sun, the moon, the stars, the ground. Noise is but interrupted silence. Hear the silence of history, of death, the silence of clouds, of snow, the silence of flowers, of all growing things, of trees, mountains, dawn, sunset. Hear the silence of candles burning, the silence of cemeteries, the silence of God, nature, people; of love, grace, sacrifice; the silence of Eucharist. Silence is the special sacrament of God's presence.[33]

Quiet Prayer

Scripture

A spirit glided past my face; the hair of my flesh bristled. It stood still, but I could not discern its appearance. A form was before my eyes; there was silence, then I heard a voice. *(Job 4:15-16)*

Then Job answered the Lord: 'See, I am of small account; what shall I answer you? I lay my hand on my mouth. I have spoken once, and I will not answer; twice, but will proceed no further.' *(Job 40:3-5)*

... without a word, without a sound, without a voice being heard, yet their message fills the world, their news reaches its rim. *(Psalm 19:4-5)*

It is good that one should wait quietly for the salvation of the Lord. It is good... to sit alone in silence when the Lord has imposed it. *(Lamentations 3:26-28)*

But the Lord is in his holy temple; let all the earth keep silence before him! *(Habakkuk 2:20)*

But when he was accused by the chief priests and elders, he did not answer. Then Pilate said to him, 'Do you not hear how many accusations they make against you?' But he gave him no answer, not even to a single charge, so that the govenor was greatly amazed. *(Matthew 27:12-14)*

Shared Prayer

Concluding Prayer

We bless you, Lord, for this time of silence
and for the space and peace it brings.
Help us to treasure the precious gift of silence
and to resist the temptation of putting it off till later.
As we discover you in the times of silence,
may our lives be blessed with new depth and tranquillity. Amen.

---

33 Edward Farrell, *Celtic Meditations* (Denville NJ: Dimension Books, 1976), 43-44

Rekindling Commitment

I remind you to rekindle the gift of God that is within you ...
for God did not give us a spirit of cowardice,
but rather a spirit of power and love and self-discipline.
(2 Timothy 1:6-7)

Focusing

Scripture

To the angel of the church in Ephesus write: These are the words of him
who holds the seven stars in his right hand, who walks among the seven
golden lampstands: 'I know your works, your toil and your patient
endurance ... I also know that you are enduring patiently and bearing up
for the sake of my name, and that you have not grown weary. But I have
this against you, that you have abandoned the love you had at first ...'

And to the angel of the church in Sardis ... 'I know your works; you
have a name of being alive, but you are dead. Wake up, and strengthen
what remains and is on the point of death ...'

And to the angel of the church in Laodicea ... 'I know your works; you
are neither cold nor hot. I wish that were either cold or hot. So, because
you are lukewarm, and neither cold nor hot, I am about to spit you out
of my mouth...'

'Be earnest, therefore, and repent ... Let anyone who has an ear to hear
listen to what the Spirit is saying to the churches.' *(Revelation 2:1-3:22)*

Meditation

Commitment begins in *love*. As Jesus said to Peter, 'Do you love me?' so our gospel commitment is founded in our ever deepening love for Jesus.

Commitment is nourished by *memory*. It means frequently going back over the life, death and resurrection of Jesus, our inspiration and hope. It means often bringing back to mind our original enthusiasm for our calling. Commitment is fired by *passion*. When we think upon our passionate God, the same passion stirs in our hearts; we feel God's own feelings for all God's creature and all God's creation.

Commitment is sustained by *courage*. It understands that things were never going to be easy and so it trusts in the Spirit's gift of courage to help it be patient and endure, awaiting with confidence the providence of the Lord.

Commitment is lived in *solidarity*. To be called is to be gathered, to struggle is to struggle together. Commitment finds its hope and energy in the sharing of vision and experience between disciples.

Commitment is carried along by *joy*. At its core, it is a deep appreciation that the gospel is good news, indeed the best news the world could ever know.

Quiet Prayer/Shared Prayer

Concluding Prayer

I bind me today
God's might to direct me,
God's power to protect me,
God's wisdom for learning,
God's eye for discerning.
(St Patrick's Breastplate)

The Long View

Focusing

Scripture

'Be patient, therefore, beloved, until the coming of the Lord.
The farmer waits for the precious crop from the earth,
being patient with it until it receives the early and the late rains.
You also must be patient.' *(James 5:7)*

Reflection

It helps now and then to step back
and take the long view.
The kingdom is not only beyond our efforts;
it is even beyond our vision.

We accomplish in our lifetime only a tiny fraction
of the magnificent enterprise that is God's work.
Nothing we do is complete,
which is another way of saying that
the kingdom always lies beyond us.
No statement says all that could be said.
No prayer fully expresses our faith.
No confession brings wholeness.
No programme accomplishes the church's mission.
No set of goals and objectives includes everything.

This is what we are about.
We plant the seeds that one day will grow.
We water seeds already planted,
knowing that they hold future promise.

We lay foundations that will need further development.
We provide yeast that produces effects
far beyond our capabilities.

We cannot do everything,
and there is a sense of liberation in realising that.
This enables us to do something, and to do it very well.
It may be incomplete, but it is a beginning,
a step along the way, an opportunity for
the Lord's grace to enter and do the rest.

We may never see the end results
but that is the difference
between the master builder and the worker.
We are workers, not master builders,
ministers, not messiahs.
We are prophets of a future not our own. Amen.
(Oscar Romero)

Quiet Prayer

Shared Prayers/Reflections

Concluding Prayer

May the brilliance of God's wisdom never fade in our eyes;
may we who love her see her with ease;
may we who seek her find her readily;
may she make herself known, anticipating us who desire her.
(Based on Wisdom 6:12-13)

God in Every Creature

Apprehend God in all things
for God is in all things
Every single creature is full of God
and is a book about God
If I spent enough time with the tiniest creature
even a caterpillar
I would never have to prepare a sermon
so full of God is every creature.
(Meister Eckhart)

Focusing

Meditation

May every creature abound
In well-being and in peace.

May every living being, weak or strong
The long and the small,
The short and the medium-sized,
The mean and the great.

May every living being, seen and unseen,
Those dwelling far-off, those near-by,
Those already born, those waiting to be born
May all attain inward peace.

Let no one deceive another
Let no one despise another in any situation
Let no one from antipathy or hatred
Wish evil to anyone at all.

Just as a mother with her own life
Protects her child, her only child, from hurt,
So within your own self foster
A limitless concern for every living creature.

Display a heart of boundless love
For all the world
In all its height and depth and broad extent,
Love unrestrained, without hate or enmity.
Then as you stand or walk, sit or lie,
until overcome by drowsiness,
Devote your mind entirely to this.
It is known as living here a life divine.
*(Buddhist prayer)*34

Quiet Prayer

Shared Prayers/Reflections

Concluding Prayer

Lord, you are love,
teach us to become loving.
Lord, you are compassion,
teach us to become compassionate.
Lord, you are gentleness,
teach us to become gentle.
Lord, you are divine,
draw us into your divinity.

---

34 Sutta-Nipata, 'A Buddhist hymn to love.' Quoted in Thomas Berry, *Buddhism* (New York: Thomas Crowell, 1975). 40-41

Hear the Bird Sing

God is the dancer
creation the dance
Be silent and contemplate the dance
Just look ...
a star, a flower, a leaf, a bird, a stone
Look, listen, touch, taste, smell ...
it won't be long before you meet
the dancer in the dance.

Focusing

Meditation

The disciple was always complaining to his Master,
"You are hiding the final secret of Zen from me.'
And he would not accept the Master's denials.

One day they were walking in the hills
when they heard a bird sing.

'Did you hear that bird sing?'
said the Master.

'Yes,' said the disciple.

'Well, now you know that I have hidden nothing from you.'

'Yes.'[35]

Quiet Prayer

If you really heard a bird sing ...
if you really saw a tree ...
you would know.
Did your heart ever fill with wordless wonder
when you heard a bird in song?

Shared Prayer/Shared Reflections

Concluding Prayer

Glorious God, so distant and so near,
open our hearts to what we know.
Lead us beyond what we seek to know
and back to what we already know.
Teach us to be still,
to be present to what is about us,
and in that stillness and presence
to know that you are God.

---

35 Anthony de Mello, *The Song of the Bird*, 16-17

Christ Before, Behind and Around

As my soul grows quiet
I return to that astounding truth
that at the heart of my being
I am eternally loved ...
I rest in your embrace.

Focusing

Reflection

Birth is a beginning and death a destination.
And life is a journey from childhood to maturity,
from youth to age;
from innocence to awareness,
from ignorance to knowing;
from foolishness to discretion
and then, perhaps, to wisdom;
from weakness to strength
or strength to weakness – and back again;
from health to sickness
and back, we pray, to health again;
from offence to forgiveness, from loneliness to love;
from joy to gratitude, from pain to compassion;
from grief to understanding, from fear to faith;
from defeat to defeat to defeat ...
Until looking backward or ahead, we see that victory lies
not at some high place along the way
but in having made the journey, stage by stage
(Hebrew prayer)

Scripture

Have no dread or fear of them.
The Lord your God, who goes before you,
is the one who will fight for you,
just as he did for you in Egypt before your very eyes,
and in the wilderness, where you saw
how the Lord your God carried you,
just as one carries a child,
all the way that you travelled until you reached this place.
(Deuteronomy 1:29-31)

For you are a people holy to the Lord your God;
the Lord your God has chosen you
out of all the people on the earth
to be his people, his treasured possession.
It was not because you were more numerous
than any other people that the Lord set his heart on you
– for you were the fewest of all peoples.
It was because the Lord loved you.
(Deuteronomy 7:6-8)

Quiet Prayer

Share Reflections/Intercessions

Concluding Prayer

Christ near, Christ here,
Christ be with me, Christ beneath me,
Christ within me, Christ behind me,
Christ be over me, Christ before me.
(St Patrick's Breastplate)

Sing God's Praise

From the stillness of a new morning
from the first call of the bird at daybreak
from the arising moment of a child's outstretch to its mother
to the surrendering murmur of night farewell
to the weary, downward slump of slumber
to the goodbye moment of day's perfect end
we sing forever God's praise.

Focusing

The One

Green, blue, yellow and red –
God is down in the swamps and marshes
Sensational as April and almost incredible the flowering of our catharsis.
A humble scene in a backward place
Where no one important ever looked
The raving flowers looked up in the face
Of the One and the Endless, the Mind that has baulked
The profoundest of mortals. A primrose, a violet,
A violent wild iris – but mostly anonymous performers
Yet an important occasion as the Muse at her toilet
Prepared to inform the local farmers
That beautiful, beautiful, beautiful God
Was breathing his love by a cut-away bog.[36]

Scripture

At that time Jesus said,
'I thank you Father, Lord of heaven and earth,
because you have hidden these things
from the wise and the intelligent
and have revealed them to infants;
yes, Father, for such was your gracious will.' *(Matthew 11:25-26)*

Quiet Prayer/Shared Reflections

Litany of Praise

Response: Blessed be God forever

God of life, the beauty and uniqueness of creation
reveals your enduring love for us.
Give us eyes to recognise your presence all about us.
Response: Blessed be God forever

God of peace, you passionately desire harmony among your creatures.
Fill us with your passion,
that we may instruments of peace in your world.
Blessed be God forever

God of wonder, the mystery of creation is beyond our understanding.
Give us the wisdom to accept humbly
the many gifts you have created for us.
Blessed be God forever

God of all ages, you have promised to be with us always.
In the despairing moments in our world,
remind us of that promise and the hope stirs up in us.
Blessed be God forever

God of the Trinity, Eternal Source of all Being,
Word of Life and Holy Spirit,
you embrace all creation and call us into relationship with you.
May we never cease to wonder at the marvel of our calling,
as we praise your glory for ever.
Blessed be God forever

Glory be ...

---

36 Patrick Kavanagh, *Selected Poems* (London: Penguin, 1966), 131

The Church as Home

'Home is the place where, when you have to go there,
they have to take you in.'
'I should have called it
something you somehow haven't to deserve.'
(Robert Frost)

Focusing

Scripture

Jesus answered him, 'Those who love me will keep my word,
and my Father will love them, and we will come to them
and make our home with them.'
(John 14:23)

Listen! I am standing at the door, knocking;
if you hear my voice and open the door
I will come in to you and eat with you, and you with me.
(Revelation 3:20)

Reflection

The indignity of homelessness has come in recent years to affect our
consciences. The homelessness of young people in the city; the homelessness of whole communities in refugee shelters; the homelessness of many
forgotten in nursing homes and mental institutions. At the same time,
this indignation brings to consciousness a further concern, namely, the
manner in which many in our society who apparently live quite normal,
secure lives, are deeply homeless in a spiritual way. Many who have a
physical home to go to have no spiritual home, no place of enduring
meaning and ultimate tranquillity where they can find rest.

The church of Jesus Christ is called to be a home for its members. Just as a physical home offers both security and acceptance, so the Christian community is to be a place where people know they are loved in themselves, a place where they experience understanding and toleration, a place of reconciliation when they yearn to return. It is to be place where their deepest questions and unrest about life and its direction are taken up into a context of hope and affirmation.

Perhaps the most powerful symbol of this church is Luke's parable of the prodigal son, a symbolism recreated in Rembrandt's painting of the encounter of son and father. But the parable has an edge, in that it symbolises two opposing possibilities for the church. In the father is symbolised the church as home, offering haven to the troubled or wayward spirit. But in the elder son there is symbolised a church that is numb, not unlike the culture we live in today, where the thirst of the spirit for home is left unquenched. The parable thus presents the church with the challenge to conversion, to turn away from the ways in which it images the elder son, to turn towards the church symbolised by the Father.

Quiet Prayer/Shared Prayer

Concluding Prayer

Lord, protect us, your pilgrim people.
As we journey towards our home in heaven,
bless us with a sense of adventure and a sense of security.
As we seek to be home-makers here on earth,
both with our loved ones and in our parish community,
may we create for each other an experience of Christian welcome
that puts us in touch with you
and gives us a foretaste of what home will be like for ever.

A Youthful Heart

Truly, I tell you, unless you change and become like children,
you will never enter the kingdom of heaven. (Matthew 18:3)

Focusing

Reflection

Youth is not a time of life, it is a state of mind;
it is a temper of the will,
a quality of the imagination,
a vigour of the emotions,
a predominance of courage over timidity,
of the appetite for adventure over love of ease.

Nobody grows old merely by living a number of years,
people grow old only by deserting their ideals.
Years wrinkle the skin,
but to give up enthusiasm wrinkles the soul.
Worry, doubt, self-distrust, fear and despair,
these are the long, long years that bow the head
and turn the growing spirit back to dust.

Whether seventy or sixteen
there is in every being's heart the love of wonder,
the sweet amazement of the stars
and the starlike things and thoughts,
the undaunted challenge of events,
the unfailing childlike appetite for what is next,
and the joy and the game of life.

You are as young as your faith, as old as your doubt;
as young as your self-confidence, as old as your fear;
as young as your hope, as old as your despair.

So long as your heart receives messages
of beauty, cheer, courage, grandeur and power
from the earth,
from the other,
from the infinite,
so long are you young.

When the wires are all down
and all the central place of your heart is covered
with the snow of pessimism and the ice of cynicism,
then you are grown old indeed,
and may God have mercy on your soul.

Quiet Prayer

Shared Reflections/Prayers

Concluding Prayer
May the Spirit of the living God renew our souls.
May the Spirit of the risen Christ
keep ever alive in us our enthusiasm for the gospel.
May the Spirit who makes all things new
protect us from losing heart.
In this Spirit may we go on rediscovering and recreating
the joy of Christ in the world. Amen.

In this Place

Then Jacob woke from his sleep and said,
'Surely the Lord is in this place – and I did not know it!'
(Genesis 28:16)

Focusing

In this place
Find a sense of
Church
Community
Communion

Hear a call to
Loving Kindness
Compassion
Unity

Know a time for
Believing
Supporting
Upholding

Recognise a feeling of
Openness
Integrity
Truthfulness

Expect a movement to
Encourage
Include
Forgive

Experience a house for
Prayer
People
God
Inhabit a haven for
The Weak
The Peacemakers
The Spirit.[37]

Scripture

So then you are no longer strangers and aliens,
but you are citizens with the saints
and also members of the household of God,
built upon the foundation of the apostles and prophets,
with Christ Jesus himself as the cornerstone.
In him the whole structure is joined together
and grows into a holy temple in the Lord;
in whom you also are built together spiritually
into a dwelling place for God.
(Ephesians 2: 19-22)

Quiet Prayer/Shared Prayer

Concluding Prayer

Dream your dream in us, O Lord,
that in this place we call church
your reign will take shape
and your people will be transformed by joy.
Glory be ...

---

37 Maureen Farrell (published with permission).

The Middle-Time

O spring in the desert,
O shelter from the heat,
O light in the darkness,
O guide for the feet,
O joy in our sadness,
O support for the weak,
O Lord with us always,
Your presence we seek.[38]

Focusing

Reflection

Between the exhilaration of Beginning
and the satisfaction of Concluding
is the Middle-Time
of Enduring … Changing … Trying …
Despairing … Continuing … Becoming.

Jesus was the person of God's Middle-Time
between Creation and Accomplishment.
Through him God said of Creation 'without Mistake'
and of Accomplishment 'without Doubt.'

And we in our Middle-Times
of Wondering and Waiting
Hurrying and Hesitating
Regretting and Revising –
we who have begun many things
and seen but few completed –

we who are becoming more, and less,
through the evidence of God's Middle-Time –
have a stabilising hint
that we are not mistakes,
that we are irreplaceable,
that our Being is of interest
and our Doing of purpose,
that our Being and Doing are surrounded by Amen.
Jesus Christ is the Completer of unfinished people
with unfinished work in unfinished times.
May he keep us from sinking, from ceasing,
from wasting, from solidifying,
that we may be for him
Experimenters, Enablers, Encouragers
and Associates in Accomplishment.

Quiet Prayer/Shared Prayer

Concluding Prayer
Lord of time and of timelessness
we look back with gratitude
at what you have done for us in Jesus your Messiah.
We look forward in anticipation
for the completion of what you have begun in him.
We look around in awareness
eager to respond to the signs of hope in our midst.

---

38 David Adam, *Tides and Seasons*, 122

The Journey Inwards

Focusing

Deep peace of the running wave to you
Deep peace of the flowing air to you
Deep peace of the quiet earth to you
Deep peace of the shining stars to you
Deep peace of the Son of peace to you.
(Iona Community)

Guided Meditation

I sit before you, Lord, upright and relaxed, with a straight spine,
allowing my weight to descend vertically through my body
to the ground on which I am sitting.
I fix my mind within my body. I resist that urge of my mind
to career out of the window to every other place but this one,
and to career forwards and backwards in time away from the present.
Gently and firmly I keep my mind where my body is – here in this room.

In this present moment I let go all plans, worries, anxieties.
I place them now in your hands, O Lord.
I release my grip on them and allow you to take them over.
For the moment I leave them to you.
I wait on you, passive and expectant.
You come towards me, and I let you carry me.

I begin the journey inwards.
I travel down inside me to the inmost core of my being, where you dwell.
In this deep centre of my being you are there before me,
ceaselessly creating and energising my whole person.

You, God, are dynamic. You are within me.
You are here. You are now. You are.
You are the ground of my being. I let go. I sink and merge into you.
You overwhelm me. You flood my being. You take me over completely.

I let my breathing become this prayer of submission to you.
My breathing, in and out, is the expression of my whole being.
I do it for you, with you, in you. I have 'become' you.
You have 'become' me.
We breathe together.

And now I open my eyes to see you in the world of things and people.
I resume responsibility for my future.
I take up again my plans, worries, anxieties.
Renewed in strength, I go again on the journey outwards,
no longer alone, but in partnership with you, the Creator.[39]

Quiet Prayer/Shared Prayer

Concluding Prayer

Lord, bless our time together.
United in fellowship, we will work in your service,
transcending envy and resentment,
calling forth the giftedness of one another.
Listening to one another,
may we hear the inspiring voice of your Spirit
and grow in the transforming power you have breathed among us.

---

39 John Dalrymple, *The Longest Journey: Notes on Christian Maturity*, (London: Darton, Longman and Todd, 1979), 101-102

Courage to Enter In

You who are my life, my very being,
my peace and my joy;
You who are my hope, my wealth and my strength;
I bow before you at this new moment in your time.
You are my home, my place of rest,
my heaven, my salvation.
You are the source of all the work of my hands,
of all the gifts of what has been,
of all the opportunities of what will be.
Keep me, Lord, in your grace.

Focusing

Scripture

And early in the morning, he came walking toward them on the sea. But when the disciples saw him walking on the sea, they were terrified, saying, 'It is a ghost!' And they cried out in fear. But immediately Jesus spoke to them and said, 'Take heart, it is I; do not be afraid.' Peter answered him, 'Lord, if it is you, command me to come to you on the water.' He said, 'Come.' So Peter got out of the boat, started walking on the water, and came toward Jesus. But when he noticed the strong wind, he became frightened, and beginning to sink, he cried out, 'Lord, save me!' Jesus immediately reached out his hand and caught him, saying to him, 'You of little faith, why did you doubt?' *(Matthew 14:25-31)*

Quiet Prayer

Intercessions

Give us, Lord, the courage to enter into this moment in time,
into this gathering of your disciples,
into this time of grace.
Lord, give us courage to enter in.

Give us, Lord, the courage to enter into the possibilities that lie before us,
like shells on the seashore,
waiting to be discovered.
Lord, give us courage to enter in.

Give us, Lord, the courage to enter into the tasks and challenges before us,
in a spirit of exploration and generosity,
in the Spirit of your Son.
Lord, give us courage to enter in.

Give us, Lord, the courage
to enter into the ideas and suggestions to be voiced
and to hear them with an open, receptive ear,
alive to the wisdom they contain.
Lord, give us courage to enter in.

Give us, Lord, the courage to enter into your presence,
to be carried along by your power,
reaching out to save us.
Lord, give us courage to enter in.

Blessing

May not the grass that grows
Nor the sand on the shore
Nor the dew on the pasture
be more plentiful than
the blessing of the King of grace
on every soul that was,
that is and that will be. *(Traditional)*

A Parable for today's Church

Focusing

Consequently I rejoice, having to construct something upon which to rejoice.
(T.S. Eliot)

Scripture

See, I am sending you out like sheep into the midst of wolves; so be wise as serpents and innocent as doves. Beware of them, for they will hand you over to councils and flog you in their synagogues; and you will be dragged before governors and kings because of me, as a testimony to them and the Gentiles. When they hand you over, do not worry about how you are to speak or what you are to say; for what you are to say will be given to you at that time; for it is not you who speak, but the Spirit of your Father speaking through you. *(Matthew 10:16-20)*

Reflection

It was time for the travellers to move out from the safety of the hut. The hut they were in was familiar and well-lit, but they knew that it could no longer serve them. It was time to venture out into dark and unfamiliar terrain, to seek out a new place of life. As they moved away from the hut, the light its windows cast on the world outside grew dim, until there was very little to guide them. They had to move along tentatively. The directions they decided on were often mistaken and they had to rely on each other for any progress they made.

Not all shared the same feelings about what they were undertaking. Where one grew frustrated, another continued to trust. Where one took heart from the adventure, another started to turn back to the light of the hut. It was a strange and unprecedented situation for them all. The only ones who knew where they were going were the ones who turned back, for they were turning to light and familiarity. But anyone embracing the future was at a loss. The only knowledge they possessed was the wisdom that accumulated as they explored their way forward.

This parable speaks to today's church. A time of safety and certainty has come to an end. A routine and predictable way of doing things has ceased to be serviceable. We are in a new situation and do not know what to do, because we have not had such an experience before. We are all at a loss. The only ones who know where they are going are the ones reaching back into the past. Those who look to the future, who wish to explore, must trust instead that moving on out in the power of the Spirit will yield its own wisdom. At first the wisdom will be very little and a bit all over the place, but slowly it will form sure patterns. But there is no way to prove this to those who stand hesitating in the doorway of the hut.

Quiet Prayer/Shared Prayer

Concluding Prayer
Blessed be the Lord, the creator, the God of the future.
Blessed be Jesus, the one who weaves God's future.
Blessed be his vision, speaking to us of new wineskins.
Blessed be his courage in stepping beyond the familiar.
Blessed be his trust in the desolation of his dying.
Blessed be the Spirit, the outpouring of Jesus' rising,
making all weary pilgrims new.
Glory be to the Father and to the Son and to the Holy Spirit.
As it was in the beginning, is now and ever shall be,
world without end. Amen.

Dying to Live your Life

Focusing

Unless a grain of wheat falls into the ground and dies, it remains just a single grain; but if it dies it bears much fruit. Those who love their life lose it, and those who hate their life in this world will keep it for eternal life.
(John 12:24-25)

Scripture

Let the same mind be in you as was in Christ Jesus, who, though he was in the form of God, did not regard equality with God as something to be exploited, but emptied himself, taking the form of a slave, being born in human likeness. And being found in human form, he humbled himself and became obedient to the point of death – even death on a cross. Therefore God also highly exalted him ... *(Philippians 2:5-9)*

Bamboo: An Indian Legend

Once upon a time there was a beautiful garden. Of all the dwellers of the garden, the most beautiful and beloved was a gracious and noble Bamboo. Year after year, Bamboo grew more beautiful and gracious. Often when the Wind came to revel in the garden, Bamboo would toss aside his dignity. He would dance and sway merrily, tossing and leaping and bowing in joyous abandon. He would lead the great dance of the garden, which most delighted his master's heart.

One day the master himself drew near. Bamboo bowed his head to the ground in joyful greeting. The master spoke: 'Bamboo, I would use you.' Bamboo flung his head to the sky in utter delight. 'Master, I am ready, use me as you want.' 'Bamboo,' the master's voice was grave, 'I would be obliged to take you and cut you down.' A trembling of great horror shook Bamboo. 'Cut ... me ... down? Ah, not that; use me for your joy,

O master, but cut me not down.' 'Beloved Bamboo, if I do not cut you down, then I cannot use you.' The garden grew still. Wind held her breath. Bamboo slowly bent his proud and glorious head. There came a whisper. 'Master, if you cannot use me unless you cut me down, then do your will and cut.'

'Bamboo, beloved Bamboo, I would cut your leaves and branches from you also.' 'Master, master, spare me. Cut me down and lay my beauty in the dust, but would you take from me my leaves and branches also?' 'Alas, if I do not cut them away, I cannot use you.' The sun hid her face. A listening butterfly glided fearfully away. Bamboo shivered in terrible expectancy, whispering low. 'Master, cut away.' 'Bamboo, Bamboo, I would divide you in two and cut out your heart, for if I do not cut so, I cannot use you.' 'Master, master, then cut and divide.'

So the master cut down Bamboo and chopped off his branches and stripped off his leaves and divided him in two and cut out his heart and, lifting him gently, carried him to a spring of fresh, sparkling water in the midst of the dry fields. He put down one end of broken Bamboo into the spring and the other end into the water channel in the field. The spring sang welcome. The clear sparkling water raced joyously down the channel of Bamboo's torn body into the waiting fields. Then the rice was planted and the days went by. The shoots grew. The harvest came. In that day was Bamboo, once so glorious in his stately beauty, yet more glorious in his brokenness and humility. For in his beauty he was life abundant. But in his brokenness he became a channel of abundant life to his master's world.[40]

Quiet Time/Shared Prayer

Concluding Prayer
We adore you, God our Father,
through Jesus Christ your Son and our brother,
who died his death so that we might live his life.
Glory be…

---

40 Told by Donal O'Leary in *Year of the Heart*, 85ff

Gifts in the Group

N.B. This exercise takes time.
If there are ten people in the group, it will take about twenty minutes.
If there are twenty people, it will take a half-hour or more.
So it is important to carry out the group discussion,
which is essentially meditative, as expeditiously as possible!

Focusing

Scripture

Do nothing from selfish ambition or conceit,
but in humility regard others as better than yourselves ...
Let the same mind be in you that was in Christ Jesus
(Philippians 2:3, 5)

For by the grace given to me I say to everyone among you
not to think of yourself more highly than you ought to think,
but to think with sober judgment,
each according to the measure of faith that God has assigned.
For, as in one body we have many members,
and not all the members have the same function,
so we, who are many, are one body in Christ,
and individually we are members one of another.
We have gifts that differ according to the grace given to us:
prophecy, in proportion to faith;
ministry, in ministering;
the teacher, in teaching;
the exhorter, in exhortation;
the giver, in generosity;
the leader, in diligence;
the compassionate, in cheerfulness.
(Romans 12:3-9)

Pause for Reflection

Group Exercise

Divide into two groups.
Each group is to discuss the gifts/giftedness
of each member of the other group.

Let a different person in the group note the gifts
of each person in the other group.
(Give two minutes per person).

When the group discussion is completed,
each person makes their presentation
(Allow five to ten minutes for presentations).

Concluding Prayer

We thank you, Lord, for the giftedness
with which you have blessed each one of us.
We pray for an open heart,
glad to appreciate the riches amongst us.
We pray that we may build on what we are,
to the realisation of your reign.
We make this prayer in the name of Jesus the Lord. Amen.

Checking in with the Group

The idea of this prayer is to give an opportunity for each member of the group to check in with the rest about how the work is going for him/her. For some the work may be fulfilling at the moment; for others frustrating; for others again there may be little or nothing to report.
Sometimes groups can lose sight of where individual members are; this prayer provides a way of addressing this concern.

Focusing

Light a big candle. Opening prayer:

We gather as a group to do the work of the Lord.
In this prayer, where we will attend to how
each of us is finding this work at the moment,
we begin by attending to the Lord of the work.
We open our hearts to the risen Jesus,
who enlightens our lives and kindles within us the fire of the Spirit.

Scripture

I want to know Christ and the power of his resurrection
and the sharing of his sufferings by becoming like him in his death,
if somehow I may attain the resurrection from the dead.
Not that I have already obtained this or have already reached the goal;
but I press on to make it my own,
because Christ Jesus has made me his own …
this one thing I do; forgetting what lies behind
and straining forward to what lies ahead,
I press on toward the goal for the prize
of the heavenly call of God in Christ Jesus.
(Philippians 3:10-14)

Quiet Time

Time for each person to reflect on his or her particular experience of the work of the group, e.g., how it's going, moments of joy and rejoicing, moments of struggle, moments of confusion, moments of learning ...

Sharing

Time for those who wish to, to share briefly on where they are at.
Each person who shares ends by lighting a small candle from the big one, while saying the prayer:

Lord. shine light on my path;
put hope in my heart;
bring fruit to my work.

Concluding Prayer

That the Lord may bless us in our work
and help us to support and encourage one another, we pray:

Our Father ...

Hail Mary ...

Glory be ...

Growing as a Group

To live is to change
and to be perfect is to have changed often
(John Henry Newman)

Focusing

Scripture

And he was transfigured before them,
and his face shone like the sun,
and his clothes became dazzling white.
Suddenly there appeared to them
Moses and Elijah, talking with him.
Then Peter said to Jesus,
'Lord, it is good for us to be here;
if you wish, I will make three dwellings here,
one for you, one for Moses, and one for Elijah.'
(Matthew 17:2-4)

Reflection

I often wonder what my reaction would have been on the mountain with
Jesus. And I have to admit that I can see the temptation of the response
of Peter. What a wonderful moment of insight and realisation it must
have been! How things must have changed in the eyes of the disciples!
Suddenly everything was so clear, the idenity of the who they were
following was so obvious. They had reached a moment of arrival. Why go
on? Why come down from this wonderful place? Why move on to a
place where things may be a bit less clear, a bit more unknowable? Why
not pitch a tent and just stop!

But God desires more than that for us. We are called to come down from the mountain, so that we may grow and flourish even more. Arrival moments are but that – moments. They are not meant to be held on to tightly, for in the tightness of our grip we may discover that what we hold dies. If we choose to move forward, if we are open to the possibilities of new discoveries and experiences, then we allow God's spirit to continue to breathe through us – bringing us deeper and deeper into God's plan for us.

Questions for Reflection

Are we as a group being called to take new steps,
or to move out in new directions?
What hopes have I for our group in the coming months?

Shared Reflections/Prayers

Concluding Prayer

Christ be with us, Christ within us,
Christ behind us, Christ before us,
In the path we take, Christ walk with us,
On the road we tread, Christ go before us.
Be a lamp for our steps and a beacon for our eyes,
that we may know through change and growth
the presence of the One who has said,
I am with you always. Amen

Gospel Mysteries of Vocation

Focusing

The Mystery of Attraction

Reader: The two disciples heard him say this, and they followed Jesus. When Jesus turned and saw them following, he said to them, 'What are you looking for?' They said to him, 'Rabbi (which translated means Teacher), where are you staying?' He said to them, 'Come and see.' They came and saw where he was staying, and they remained with him that day. *(John 1:37-39)*

Our Father ... Hail Mary ... Glory Be ...
All: Lord, may each day bring a new freshness in our relationship with you.

The Mystery of Courage

Reader: Jesus spoke to them and said, 'Take heart, it is I; do not be afraid.' Peter answered him, 'Lord, if it is you, command me to come to you on the water.' He said, 'Come.' So Peter got out of the boat, started walking on the water and came toward Jesus. But when he noticed the strong wind, he became frightened, and beginning to sink, he cried out, 'Lord save me!' Jesus immediately reached out his hand and caught him, saying to him, 'You of little faith, why did you doubt?' *(Matthew 14:27-31)*

Our Father ... Hail Mary ... Glory Be ...
All: Lord, confirm us in our courage, hearten us in our fears.

The Mystery of Compassion

Reader: And they went away in the boat to a deserted place by them-selves. Now many saw them going and recognised them and they hurried there on foot from all the towns and arrived ahead of them. As he went ashore, he saw a great crowd; and he had compassion for them, because they were like sheep without a shepherd; and he began to teach them many things. *(Mark 6:32-34)*

Our Father ... Hail Mary ... Glory Be ...
All: Lord, give us the grace of feeling your feelings for God's people.

The Mystery of Mission

Reader: After this the Lord appointed seventy others and sent them on ahead of him in pairs to every town and place where he himself intended to go. He said to them, 'The harvest is plentiful, but the labourers are few; therefore ask the Lord of the harvest to send out labourers into his harvest.' *(Luke 10:1-2)*

Our Father ... Hail Mary ... Glory Be ...
All: Lord, send us forth and give success to the work of our hands.

The Mystery of Love

Reader: He said to him the third time, 'Simon son of John, do you love me?' Peter felt hurt because he said to him the third time, 'Do you love me?' And he said to him, 'Lord you know everything, you know that I love you.' Jesus said to him, 'Feed my sheep.' ... After this he said to him, 'Follow me.' *(John 21:17-19)*

Our Father ... Hail Mary ... Glory Be ...
All: Lord, you know everything, you know that I love you.[41]

---

41 Donal Harrington, *Parish Renewal*, Vol. II: Resources (Dublin: Columba, 1997), 187

Gospel Mysteries of Community

Focusing

The Mystery of Presence

Reader: For where two or three are gathered in my name, I am there among them. *(Matthew 18:20)*

Our Father ... Hail Mary ... Glory Be ...
All: Lord, give us eyes to see you present in our parish and in our fellow-parishioners.

The Mystery of Belonging

Reader: Simon Peter answered him, 'Lord, to whom can we go? You have the words of eternal life. We have come to believe and know that you are the Holy One of God.' *(John 6:68-69)*

Our Father ... Hail Mary ... Glory Be ...
All: Lord, may each person in our parish know the joy of belonging to Christian community.

The Mystery of Giftedness

Reader: There are varieties of gifts, but the same Spirit; and there are varieties of services, but the same Lord; and there are varieties of activities, but it is the same God who activates all of them in everyone. To each is given the manifestation of the Spirit for the common good. *(1 Corinthians 12:4-7)*

Our Father ... Hail Mary ... Glory Be ...
All: Lord, give each one of us in this parish a deep gratitude for how you have gifted us individually.

The Mystery of Companionship

Reader: When he was at the table with them, he took bread, blessed and broke it, and gave it to them. Then their eyes were opened, and they recognised him. *(Luke 24:30-31)*

Our Father... Hail Mary... Glory Be...
All: Lord, as we break bread together, may we grow in companionship with each other.

The Mystery of Service

Reader: After he had washed their feet ... he said to them, 'Do you know what I have done to you? You call me Teacher and Lord – and you are right, for that is what I am. So if I, your Lord and Teacher, have washed your feet, you also ought to wash one another's feet. For I have set you an example, that you also should do as I have done to you.' *(John 13:12-15)*

Our Father ... Hail Mary ... Glory Be ...
All: Lord, teach us to reach out, with a heartfelt compassion for the needs of one another.[42]

---

42 Donal Harrington, *Parish Renewal,* Vol. II: Resources (Dublin: Columba, 1997), 187

Gospel Mysteries of Mission

Focusing

The Mystery of Being Recognised

Reader: When the fulness of time had come, God sent his Son ... so that we might receive adoption as children. And because you are children, God has sent the Spirit of his Son into our hearts, crying 'Abba! Father!' So you are no longer a slave but a child, and if a child then also an heir. *(Galatians 4:4-7)*

Our Father... Hail Mary... Glory Be...
All: Lord, for the inexpressible delight of being loved eternally, we thank you.

The Mystery of New Life

Reader: He unrolled the scroll and found the place where it was written: 'The Spirit of the Lord is upon me, because he has anointed me to bring good news to the poor. He has sent me to proclaim release to the captives and recovery of sight to the blind, to let the oppressed go free, to proclaim the year of the Lord's favour.' *(Luke 4:17-19)*.

Our Father ... Hail Mary ... Glory Be ...
All: Lord, help us to reach out, that more and more people may hear good news.

The Mystery of Moving On

Reader: When they found him, they said to him, 'Everyone is searching for you.' He answered, 'Let us go on to the neighbouring towns, so that I may proclaim the message there also; for that is what I came out to do.' And he went throughout Galilee, proclaiming the message in their synagogues and casting out demons. *(Mark 1:37-39)*

Our Father ... Hail Mary ... Glory Be ...
All: Lord Jesus, sent from the Father, may all God's children feel your embrace.

The Mystery of Proclaiming

Reader: Many Samaritans from that city believed in him because of the woman's testimony, 'He told me everything I have ever done' ... They said to the woman, 'It is no longer because of what you said that we believe, for we have heard for ourselves, and we know that this is truly the Saviour of the world.' *(John 4:39-42)*

Our Father ... Hail Mary ... Glory Be ...
All: Lord, we pray that through us many others will have the experience of you.

The Mystery of the Spirit

Reader: But how are they to call on one in whom they have not believed? And how are they to believe in one of whom they have never heard? And how are they to hear without someone to proclaim him? And how are they to proclaim him unless they are sent? ... So faith comes from what is heard, and what is heard comes through the word of Christ. *(Romans 10:14-17)*

Our Father... Hail Mary... Glory Be...
All: Lord, breathe on us your Spirit, that your work may be accomplished.[43]

---

43 Donal Harrington, *Parish Renewal,* Vol. II: Resources (Dublin: Columba, 1997), 188

Begin Again

Focusing

Opening Prayer
God of faithfulness, God ever new,
as this new year brings new projects and possibilities,
we are in need of energy and renewed hope.
Wondering what change are we able to effect
by our words and actions and prayers,
we need your grace to guide our hearts.
We need the power of your Son to rekindle and sustain our passion.
We need the wisdom of your Spirit to see the ever-present possibility
for change and conversion, for growth and transformation.
Give us eyes of faith, that we might see the wonders in our midst,
that we might have the courage to hope.

> *Begin*
> *Begin again to the summmoning birds,*
> *to the sight of light at the window,*
> *begin to the roar of morning taffic*
> *all along Pembroke Road.*
> *Every beginning is a promise*
> *born in light and dying in dark*
> *determination and exaltation of Springtime*
> *flowering the way to work.*
> *Begin to the pageant of queueing girls*
> *the arrogant loneliness of swans in the canal,*
> *bridges linking the past and future,*
> *old friends passing though with us still.*
> *Begin to the loneliness that cannot end*
> *since it perhaps is what makes us begin,*

begin to wonder at unknown faces,
at crying birds in the sudden rain
at branches stark in the willing sunlight
at seagulls foraging for bread
at couples sharing a sunny secret
alone together while making good.
Though we live in a world that dreams of ending
that always seems about to give in
something that will not acknowledge conclusion
insists that we forever begin.[44]

Quiet Time

Shared Prayer

Concluding Prayer

In the light of the Father of light,
we begin to see the way forward.
In the courage of Jesus who risked everything,
we find ourselves heartened and enthused.
In the joy of the Spirit among us,
we rejoice in God's providence in our lives.

Blessed are you, eternal source of all life.
Bless are you, word of life, word of truth.
Blessed are you, creative spirit in our midst. Amen.

---

44 Brendan Kennelly (published with the permission of the author)

Prayer before a Meeting

For where two or three are gathered in my name,
I am there among them.
(Matthew 18:20)

Focusing

For the Meeting

Lord, as we prepare to begin our meeting,
we recall your promise to be present
when two or three are gathered in your name.
We know that without you here among us,
and within each one of us,
we will labour in vain.
All: Unite us, Lord, in your Spirit.

We rejoice that we are blessed and called together
to work in your name.
We pray that we will respond generously
to this opportunity to serve you
and that we will grow in our Christian calling.
All: Unite us, Lord, in your Spirit.

Inspire us with your Spirit of wisdom;
plant seeds of your vision in our hearts and minds;
give us humour and give us humility
in our working with one another,
so that we may know the privilege of participating
in the coming about of your Kingdom.
All: Unite us, Lord, in your Spirit.

We ask that working together
will increase the communion among us
as members of your Body on earth.
May the communion we experience
give us new courage in all that we do for you.
All: Unite us, Lord, in your Spirit.

Grant us the willingness to be open to each other,
to respect each other,
to listen to each other,
to be honest with each other
to be supportive of each other,
for the sake of your Kingdom.
All: Unite us, Lord, in your Spirit.

Quiet Prayer

Concluding Prayer

It is our hope that the true business of this meeting
will be our spiritual transformation
and the transformation of others through us,
and not simply the accomplishment
of tasks and projects.
We ask this of you as we now begin
in the name of the Father and of the Son and of the Holy Spirit.
Amen.[45]

---

45 Edward Hays, *Prayers for the Servants of God* (Easton KS: Forest of Peace Books, 1980), 108-109 (adapted)

Prayer for the Meeting

Focusing

The Lord of the meeting

Forgive me Lord
because while I believe with all my heart
that you need me,
need us,
to build a fraternal world
I often forget that I
cannot do it without you ...
I work alone
struggle alone
fight alone
and I'm afraid that's what others do also
because often we don't think of inviting you
to the meeting
and when we say you are there
because we are accustomed to saying it
we avoid searching for
and asking for your opinion
because it's easier to settle for our own
and more difficult to reflect on your gospel
and pray in your Spirit.
But we are building in vain Lord,
until we build with you.
You are there, Lord, and I am speaking to you ...
I entrust this meeting to you.[46]

Quiet Prayer

Scripture

Abide in me as I abide in you. Just as the branch cannot bear fruit by itself unless it abides in the vine, neither can you unless you abide in me. I am the vine, you are the branches. Those who abide in me and I in them bear much fruit, because apart from me you can do nothing. *(John 15:4-5)*

Intercessions/Reflections

Concluding Prayer

Father, breathe your Spirit
upon your people gathered together to do your work.
Grace us, we pray, with
a new sense of your mystery,
a new experience of your presence,
a new commitment to your gospel,
a new dedication to your kingdom.
May your Spirit be our inspiration
and may our work contribute to
the coming of your kingdom,
through Christ our Lord. Amen.

---

46 Dermot Dowdall and Dorothy Ng (printed with permission)

At the Beginning of the Day

In the silence of the stars, in the quiet of the hills,
In the heaving of the sea, Speak, Lord.
In the stillness of this room, in the calming of my mind,
In the longing of my heart, Speak, Lord.
In the voice of a friend, in the chatter of a child,
In the words of a stranger, Speak, Lord.
In the opening of a book, in the looking at a film,
In the listening to music, Speak, Lord
For your servant listens.[47]

Focusing

Scripture

And very early on the first day of the week, when the sun had risen, they went to the tomb. They had been saying to one another, 'Who will roll away the stone for us from the entrance of the tomb?' When they looked up, they saw that the stone, which was very large, had already been rolled back. As they entered the tomb, they saw a young man, dressed in a white robe, sitting on the right side; and they were alarmed. But he said to them, 'Do not be alarmed; you are looking for Jesus of Nazareth, who was crucified. He has been raised; he is not here.' *(Mark 16:2-6)*

On this Day

On this day, Lord, I welcome you into my heart.
I create a space within
and acknowledge your presence at the core of my being.

Thank you for the gift of this day,
for the restful sleep that has prepared me for the day's journey.
Thank you for the rising sun
that has invited me to enter into the delights that lie ahead.

As I go forth into this day
let me carry with me the joy of resurrection.
May this joy encourage me to embrace the opportunities of this day,
May it enable me to venture into the unknown, into the new,
with a courageous heart.

In my coming and in my going this day
may I greet all as Christ.
Give me the vision to see the many ways Christ will be present to me.
Let me not pass him by in stranger or in friend.
Let my words and actions today be ones directed to and inspired by Christ.

Lord, bless this day for me and for everyone,
As I begin it, mindful of the resurrection,
may I end it thankful for the life and growth
that the joy of resurrection led me to this day.

Quiet Prayer/Shared Prayer

A Blessing

May the God of new beginnings lead us forward this day
May the God who brought us new life in Christ
fill us with resurrection joy this day
May the God who abides within us be revealed to all we meet this day
May the God who consoles and protects us soothe any heartache this day
May the God who desires abundance of life for all creation
renew our spirits this day.

---

47 David Adam, *Tides and Seasons*, 13

Before Work

Focusing

> *You must bring him everything!*
> *Your dreams, your successes, your rejoicing.*
> *And if you have little to rejoice over, bring him that little.*
> *And if your life seems only like a heap of fragments,*
> *bring him the fragments.*
> *And if you have only empty hands, bring him your empty hands.*
> *Shattered hopes are his material;*
> *in his hands all is made good.*
> *(Meister Eckhart)*

Scripture

They left weeping, weeping,
casting the seed.
They come back singing, singing,
holding high the harvest. *(Psalm 126:6)*

Let your loveliness shine on us,
and bless the work we do,
bless the work of our hands. *(Psalm 90:17)*

I planted, Apollos watered, but God gave the growth.
So neither the one who plants nor the one who waters is anything,
but only God who gives the growth ...
For we are God's servants, working together. *(1 Corinthians 3:6-7, 9)*

For we are what he has made us,
created in Christ Jesus for good works. *(Ephesians 2:10)*

Meditation

Before we begin our work, we turn to you O Lord.
For it is your work that we do, the work of your gospel.
We know this but we often lose sight of it.
We begin to rely on our own efforts only.
Or we lose sight of the vision and get absorbed in the details.
And so today, we bring to our work a lively sense that you, Lord,
are the ground and the goal, the inspiration of all that we do.
In this awareness may we do our work lovingly.
In this awareness may we do our work joyfully.
May we be not too quick with our judgments,
our agenda, our interpretations.
May we pause patiently, to open up to your wisdom,
to see with your eyes.
And may we be not so absorbed in our tasks
that we forget our co-workers and those for whom we struggle.
May the way in which we carry out our work
make for healing and reassurance for all.

Quiet Prayer/Shared Prayer

Blessing

Bless us, O Lord, in our work today,
bless us, O Lord, and be with us, we pray.
May all that we do your glory proclaim,
may all that we do be done in your name.

The Circle of Seasons

11/29
RCIA

What has been is what will be,
and what has been done is what will be done;
there is nothing new under the sun.
(Ecclesiastes 1:9)

Focusing

Scripture

For everything there is a season,
a time for every occupation under heaven:
a time to be born, and a time to die;
a time to plant, and a time to pluck up what has been planted …
a time to weep, and a time to laugh;
a time to mourn, and a time to dance …
a time to seek, and a time to lose;
a time to keep, and a time to throw away.
(Ecclesiastes 3:1-6)

Your moon knows when to rise,
your sun when to set.
Your darkness brings on night
when wild beasts prowl.
The young lions roar to you
in search of prey.
They slink off to dens
to rest at daybreak,
then people rise to work
until the daylight fades.
God, how fertile your genius!
You shape each thing,
you fill the world
with what you do. *(Psalm 104:19-24)*

Reflection

You have noticed that everything an Indian does is in a circle, and that is because the Power of the World always works in circles and everything tries to be round ... The sky is round, and I have heard that the earth is round like a ball, and so are all the stars. The wind, in its greatest power, whirls. Birds make their nests in circles, for theirs is the same religion as ours. The sun comes forth and goes down again in a circle. The moon does the same, and both are round. Even the seasons form a great circle in their changing, and always come back again to where they were. The life of a man is a circle from childhood to childhood, and so it is in everything where power moves.[48]

Quiet Prayer

Share Reflections/Intercessions

Concluding Prayer

God of the seasons, you have gifted us
with their rhythm of dying and rising.
May the beauty of this rhythm find a place in our hearts,
so that it will continue to be for us a source of refreshment and renewal
as we make our journey to you.
We ask this through Christ our Lord.

---

48 John G. Neihardt, *Black Elk Speaks*, (Lincoln NE: University of Nebraska Press, 1979), 194-195.

Praise the Lord for the Seasons

Focusing

Scripture

Alleluia! Praise the Lord!
Across the heavens, from the heights,
all you angels, heavenly beings, sing praise, sing praise!
Sun and moon, glittering stars, sing praise, sing praise.
Highest heavens, rain clouds, sing praise, sing praise.
Let there be praise; from the depths of the earth,
from creatures of the deep.
Fire and hail, snow and mist, storms, winds, mountains, hills,
fruit trees and cedars, wild beasts and tame, snakes and birds ...
praise, praise the holy name, this name beyond all names.
God's splendour above the earth, above the heavens,
gives strength to the nation, glory to the faithful.
(Psalm 148:1-4, 7-10, 13-14)

Reflection

The seasons can be so hard on us. They force us to face the world as it is
– bitingly cold, swelteringly hot, unpredictable, subtle, devastating,
life-threatening even. There is no hidden shame in the seasons – they are
what they are and they stand upright, proud of their identity. As they roll
through the year they reveal, diamond-like, the many sides to wonder
and beauty. In one breath we struggle, despair, welcome back and marvel
at the intricacy of the Winter, Spring, Summer, Autumn symphony of
creation. For in the end we know that in all creation the composing hand
of God is at work – revealing, restoring and renewing God's people,
leading God's people to, in turn, be glorified through the power and
presence of God.

Quiet Prayer

Thanksgiving

Creator God, you have blessed us with the wonder of the seasons. Accept our Summer praise – for the warmth and length of days, for the times of re-creation and rest, for the colourful blooms of flowers and the refreshment of sea and lake – for all the gifts and signs of Summer we give you thanks.
Sing praise, sing praise and thanks to God our creator.

Accept our Autumn praise – for the beauty of changing colours, for the abundance of harvest and the sharing of labour, for the crispness of leaves under foot and the first wrappings of scarves and gloves – for all the gifts and signs of Autumn we give you thanks.
Sing praise, sing praise and thanks to God our creator.

Accept our Winter praise – for frost and ice, for snow and wind, for fire-time chats and warming drinks, for the experience of longing and first hints of new growth, for an earth ready and waiting to bring forth life – for all the gifts and signs of Winter we give you thanks.
Sing praise, sing praise and thanks to God our creator.

Accept our Spring praise – for the triumph of daffodils and the faltering steps of lambs, for stretches of light and the gentle beginnings of warmth, for rebirth that reminds us and invites us to resurrection – for all the gifts and signs of Spring we give you thanks.
Sing praise, sing praise and thanks to God our creator.

Concluding Prayer

God of all creation, you have gifted us with the cycles of Summer, Autumn, Winter and Spring. Just as we witness in the seasons the natural process of dying and rising, changing and renewing, may we accept the invitation into this process in our own lives. Guided by your presence, may we be open to the needs of change and thereby discover the gift of renewal. We ask this through Christ our Lord.

Advent One: An Awaiting People

Since the coming of Christ goes on forever –
he is always he who is to come in the world and in the church –
there is always an Advent going on. (Jean Danielou)

Focusing

Lighting of Advent Wreath:

Almighty God, we begin this advent season as an advent people – ready to do your will. Let your blessing come upon us as we light this wreath. May it turn our hearts to you in the days ahead. Grant us the peace and joy we long for, as we await the coming of your Son with patient hearts. We ask this through Christ our Lord.

Scripture

Be patient, therefore, beloved, until the coming of the Lord.
The farmer waits for the precious crop from the earth,
being patient with it until it receives the early and the late rains.
You also must be patient.
Strengthen your hearts, for the coming of the Lord is at hand.
(James 5:7-8)

Reflection

Advent is a waiting time,
– we await the celebration of the birth of Jesus,
– we await Christ's second coming,
– but God waits for us too.

God lives today, and so …
our first challenge is to bring Jesus to life in our own living,
to become aware of his presence,
the presence of the Spirit within us, prompting us,
sustaining us, working through us, waiting for us.

Quiet Prayer and Reflection

Intercessions

We await your coming and with joyful hearts we pray:
Come, Lord Jesus!
You come to bring us hope and courage:
May we be people of hope and courage in our world today.
You come as a reflection of God's love:
May our actions of justice and care reflect this same love.
You come to show us ways of compassion and mercy:
May we reach out to all people in our society
with that same spirit of compassion and mercy.
We await your coming and with joyful hearts we pray:
Come, Lord Jesus!

Closing Prayer

O God, open our hearts to prepare the way for the coming of Christ.
Guide us in your ways of compassion
so that we may extend your love and mercy to all people.
We ask this in the name of Jesus, the Eternal Word,
who lives with you and the Holy Spirit forever. Amen

Advent Two: Prepare the Way

Prepare the way for the Lord,
smooth the path for our God.

Focusing

Lighting of Advent Wreath
Lord God,
may the light of this wreath be a sign of hope
to all people who prepare for your coming.
Let the truth of your Word lead us all
toward your kingdom for which we long.
We ask this through Christ our Lord. Amen.

Scripture

A voice cries out:
in the wilderness prepare the way of the Lord,
make straight in the desert a highway for our God.
Every valley shall be lifted up,
and every mountain and hill be made low;
the uneven ground shall become level,
and the rough places a plain.
Then the glory of the Lord shall be revealed,
and all people shall see it together;
for the mouth of the Lord has spoken.
(Isaiah 40:3-5)

Reflection

Not too far from where I live there's a road being built, nearing completion. It's going to transform what has been a tortuous journey. The old road is a slow five mile stretch over a mountain; very hilly, very twisty, very slow. Now, as you drive the old road, you can see the new highway becoming. It's astounding, a straight way through the mountain, decisive and cutting and fast.

This is my image of what Isaiah speaks of – a highway through the wilderness, valleys filled in, mountains made low, rugged land become plain. The sweep of it! I think of my hard heart, the rugged land within, the hard rock, the uncompromising terrain. And a voice cries, 'Prepare a way for the Lord!' Who could have believed that this mountain could be cut through, a highway constructed here?

Lord, my heart is hard. It is desert weeping for water, rock needing rain. And now it hears this voice! Too wonderful for words the hope it engenders. I can marvel at the feats of modern engineering, but I gasp in silent amazement at what you, Lord, do in the bleak places of my life.

Quiet time

Shared Prayer/Reflections

Closing Prayer

Lord God, may we, your people,
who prepare a way for the Lord,
experience the joy of salvation
and celebrate the feast of Christ
with love and thanksgiving. Amen.

Staff 12/17/99 →7

Advent Three: The Reign of God's Justice

Focusing

Lighting of Advent Wreath

Almighty God, your promise of salvation fills us with joy and hope. We long for its fulfillment in our own time. Hear the cries of your people and let your justice be evident in our world, that we and all people may have ever new reasons to rejoice in your love. Through Christ our Lord.

Scripture

The days are surely coming, says the Lord, when I will fulfill the promise I made to the house of Israel and the house of Judah. In those days and at that time I will cause a righteous Branch to spring up from David; and he shall execute justice and righteousness in the land. In those days Judah will be saved and Jerusalem will live in safety. And this is the name by which it will be called: 'The Lord is our righteousness.'
(Jeremiah 33:14-16)

Meditation

You are the caller, you are the poor, you are the stranger at my door.
You are the wanderer, the unfed, you are the homeless with no bed.
You are the man driven insane, you are the child crying in pain.
You are the other who comes to me.
If I open to another you're born in me.[49]

Reflection

No one can celebrate a genuine Christmas without being truly poor. The self-sufficient, the proud, those who, because they have everything, look down on others, those who have no need even of God – for them there will be no Christmas. Only the poor, the hungry, those who need someone to come on their behalf, will have that someone. That someone is God, Emmanuel, God-with-us. Without poverty of Spirit there can be no abundance of God. *(Oscar Romero)*

Quiet Prayer and Reflection

Intercessions

O God, you joyfully embraced humanity for our sake.
With gratitude we pray:
Come, Christ our saviour!
You come into the world to bring justice and peace:
May justice and peace in our world
be the fruits of justice and peace in our hearts.
You come in the face of the stranger:
May we always have the eyes to see Christ in the unknown face.
You come in the midst of contradiction and pain:
May we reach out the gentle hand of Christ
in situations beyond our understanding.
You come in the broken body of humanity:
May we always choose to soothe rather than condemn.
O God you come as one who is with us, our Emmanuel:
May we be with and for one another,
in a spirit of solidarity and love with all God's people.

Closing Prayer

O God, your will is justice for the poor and peace for the afflicted.
May the news of the dawn of your coming
cut through our hardened hearts.
As your Jesus comes, baptising with the fire of the Spirit,
may our complacency give way to conversion.
May we cease to oppress and learn to be just.
May we cease to contend and learn to accept each other in Christ.
We ask this through him whose coming is certain, whose day draws near.
Amen.

---

49 David Adam, *The Edge of Glory – Prayers in the Celtic Tradition* (Harrisburg PA: Morehouse
Publishing, 1985), 34

12/13/00 – Deanery
(snowed out – didn't use!)

Advent Four: Together with our Ancestors

Since the coming of Christ goes on forever –
he is always he who is to come in the world and in the church –
there is always an Advent going on.
(Jean Danielou)

Focusing

Lighting of Advent Wreath

Lord God, the brightness of our wreath reflects the glory of your Son, whose coming we soon will celebrate. Let your blessing come upon us as it has come upon our ancestors in faith from age to age. We ask this through Christ our Lord. Amen.

Scripture

But you, O Bethlehem of Ephrathah,
who are one of the little clans of Judah,
from you shall come forth for me one who is to rule in Israel,
whose origin is from of old, from ancient days ...
And he shall stand and feed his flock in the strength of the Lord,
in the majesty of the name of the Lord his God.
And they shall live secure,
for now he shall be great to the ends of the earth;
and he shall be the one of peace. *(Micah 5:2, 4-5)*

In those days Mary set out and went with haste to a Judean town in the hill country, where she entered the house of Zachariah and greeted Elizabeth. When Elizabeth heard Mary's greeting, the child leaped in her womb. And Elizabeth was filled with the Holy Spirit and exclaimed with a loud cry, 'Blessed are you among women, and blessed is the fruit of your womb. And why has this happened to me, that the mother of my Lord comes to me? For as soon as I heard the sound of your greeting, the child in my womb leaped for joy. And blessed is she who believed that there would be a fulfilment of what was spoken to her by the Lord.' *(Luke 1:39-45)*

Reflection

We are the people of Advent, for Advent is now, and not just back then. Therefore we can see all the characters of the Advent that was 'then' in our Advent which is 'now'. Where in our lives is John the Baptist, provoking us to become aware of new things happening in our lives? Where is Zachariah in our lives, not immediately open to what is so new, so hard to understand? Where is Elizabeth, so ready, through the wisdom of living, to appreciate the coming of the Lord? Where is Joseph, so gracious when all was so strange? And where is Mary in us, trusting in the providence given to her, welcoming the word in her heart? For, where we find Mary in ourselves, there we find Christ being born in our souls.

Quiet Prayer & Sharing

Group Petition

In the company of Abraham and Isaac, *Deep peace of the running wave to us.*
In the company of Sarah and Hagar, *Deep peace of the flowing air to us.*
In the company of David and Hannah, *Deep peace of the quiet earth to us.*
In the company of Joseph and Zachariah, *Deep peace of the shining stars to us.*
In the company of Mary and Elizabeth, *Deep peace of the Son of peace to us.*
(Iona Community, adapted)

Closing Prayer

Blessed be the eternal God, whose promise has been taking shape for us in the events of history – in Abraham's venturing forth, in David's singing praise, in the prophet's crying out, in Mary's saying Yes. As our hearts quicken to the advent of what is promised, may Emmanuel be born in our souls and take flesh in our lives. May God-with-us be for all men and women the salvation and joy for which they long. We make this prayer in the power of the Spirit, who lives and reigns with the Father and the Son, world without end. Amen.

The Brightness of Christmas

The people who walked in darkness
have seen a great light;
those who lived in a land of deep darkness —
on them light has shined.
(Isaiah 9:2)

Focusing

Scripture

In the beginning was the Word,
and the Word was with God,
and the Word was God.
He was in the beginning with God.
All things came into being through him,
and without him not one thing came into being.
What has come into being in him was life,
and the life was the light of all people.
The light shines in the darkness,
and the darkness did not overcome it.
(John 1:1-5)

Reflection

A December day; bright blue sky. The sun is so low for daytime, addressing the world almost horizontally. And with such powerful light; total, blinding light. This day, this light, is blessed. Considering how so many find that what is most depressing about winter is the darkness – dark when we arise, dark when we return homewards – such a bright day is precious indeed.

Newgrange, so long ago we naïvely call them primitive times, primitive people. An elaborate burial chamber, adorned with a simple, profound idea. That on the winter solstice, such being the structure of the chamber, this powerful horizontal-almost winter sun would cut through an opening over the lintel and shoot straight down the corridor, to bathe in total light the chamber of the dead.

Centuries, even millennia later, Christians adorned their faith with another idea, in the same spirit of profound simplicity. They identified this winter solstice as the day on which they would celebrate the Incarnation. From now on, the day when winter sun bathes total dark in total light would be the statement of God's light drowning the darkest in human existence and human experience.

Quiet Time

Shared Prayers

Concluding Prayer
O light of God, brightest in darkest winter,
find an opening in us.
Shoot down the corridors of our being,
drench our dark souls in light,
your radiance in our lives, our world.

The New Year

Staff
1/17/0/

Focusing

Time Marches On

One of the most significant inventions of all time is the mechanical clock. To be sure, there were sand clocks and water clocks and sun clocks and candle clocks for many millennia, but with the mechanical clock the human race incorporated the night hours into its schedules. And that was momentous. For, up to that time, night was a time to eat, to tell stories, and to sleep. Jesus, living in the pre-mechanical time, makes reference to that … he says, 'Night time comes when no one can work.' Now we say, 'Work and shop until you drop' at the stores, and factories open 24 hours a day.

The mechanical clock met a need, the need of monks to pray at set times. But the clock takes on a different function today. It does not summon us to prayer, but tempts us to fill every hour, every minute and every second of our lives with a thousand bits of busy-ness that leave us no time for God, or for ourselves.

Advertisers add to the problem by compressing time for us. In July they advertise back-to-school sales; in September, Christmas gifts; at Ash Wednesday, Easter finery; in May, Summer sales. They move us constantly round and round like squirrels on a wheel, never giving us the time to savour the current celebration and mystery, in the hot economic pursuit of the next … As someone wrote in a rather cynical poem:
  This is the age of the half-read page,
  The quick hash and the mad dash.
  This is the age of the bright night and the nerves tight,
  And the plane with a brief stop.
  This is the age of the lamp tan in a short span
  The brain strain and the heart pain
  The catnaps till the spring snaps and the fun is done.[50]

Scripture

'Do not remember the former things, or consider the things of old.
I am about to do a new thing; now it springs forth,
do you not perceive it?' *(Isaiah 43:18-19).*

And the one who was seated on the throne said,
'See, I am making all things new.' *(Revelation 21:5)*

Quiet Prayer

Intercessions

Response: We bless you, Lord, for your gift of time.

With our trust in you, O Lord, we look forward to the days and weeks
and months that lie ahead, knowing that they will never fail to reveal
signs of your providence.

Rejoicing in you, O Lord, we reach out to embrace all the moments and
occasions of the coming year, knowing that they will ever surprise us with
opportunities for celebrating your salvation.

May times of happiness teach us the depth of your love. May times of
adversity teach us the reach of your care. In all times may we bless you,
Father, Son and Spirit, in whom it is our destiny to live, forever and ever.
Amen.

---

50 William Bausch, *Storytelling the Word* (Mystic, CT: Twenty-Third Publications, 1996) 212-214

Christians Growing as One

Dialogue does not extend exclusively to matters of doctrine,
but engages the whole person;
it is also a dialogue of love.
(John Paul II, Ut Unum Sint, 47)

Focusing

Scripture

For just as the body is one and has many members,
and all the members of the body,
though many, are one body,
so it is with Christ.
For in the one Spirit we were all baptised into one body
– Jews or Greeks, slaves or free –
and we were all made to drink of one Spirit.
(1 Corinthians 12: 12-13)

Reflection

When brothers and sisters who are not in perfect communion with one another come together to pray, the Second Vatican Council defines their prayer as the soul of the whole ecumenical movement. The common prayer of Christians is an invitation to Christ himself to visit the 'two or three gathered in his name'. If Christians, despite their division, can grow ever more united in common prayer around Christ, they will grow in the awareness of how little divides them in comparison to what unites them.
(John Paul II, Ut Unum Sint, 21-22)

Quiet Time

Shared Prayer/Reflections

Intercessions

Lord, help us to appreciate difference.
Take us beyond the narrow confines of uniformity,
where difference is always a threat.
Allow us to see that diversity is a gift
and that opening ourselves to the different perspectives of others
can only enhance our own faith.
Response: Bless us, Lord, with a desire for unity.

Lord, many people are afraid of our church.
People of other faiths often feel that we are more interested
in converting them than in being enriched by their fidelity.
Give us a listening heart,
to appreciate the different aspects of your mystery
that shine through in other Christian churches.
Bless us, Lord, with a desire for unity.

Lord, teach us a broader vision as we join in the renewal of your church.
In our own place, may we do what we can
to make this challenge of renewal the shared work
of all who put their hope in the power of the resurrection.
Bless us, Lord, with a desire for unity.

Glory be to the Father ...

The Kiss of Spring

Focusing

Reflection

Such is the grip of winter – we long to escape;
such is the darkness of winter – we yearn for the sun.

Yet, in the grip of darkness
restless seeds struggle towards the light;
from the darkness of the earth buds will burst forth
and dull landscapes will be splashed with colour.

Spring invites us into expectation,
kisses us in anticipation,
awakens us from the quiet months
and enlivens our yearning hearts.

As life breaks out from the earth
the Lord of Spring,
working in our hearts,
calls us to new birth.

As life breaks out from the earth
the Lord of Spring,
working in our church,
calls us to new hope.

As life breaks out from the earth
the Lord of Spring,
working in our world,
calls us to new vitality

Scripture
Very truly, I tell you,
unless a grain of wheat falls into the earth and dies,
it remains just a single grain;
but if it dies, it bears much fruit.
(John 12:24)

Quiet Time

Shared Prayer

Concluding Prayer
Teach us, O Lord, the wisdom of Spring,
and release our souls from the grip of Winter.
Give us the restlessness of the bursting bud,
the joy of bursting forth and bearing fruit.
May our beings thrill in harmony with nature,
with the vitality of new birth.
We make this prayer through Jesus your Son,
who brings Spring into our lives
and life into our Spring.

St Brigid (February 1)

I bind myself to the mind and heart of Brigid this day.
With the daughter of Ireland,
in the company of my brothers and sisters in Christ,
I journey towards my God in prayer ...

Focusing

Brigid's Feast

I should like a great lake of finest ale
for the King of Kings.
I should like a table of choicest food
for the Family of Heaven.
Let the ale be made from the fruits of faith,
And the food be forgiving love.

I should welcome the poor to my feast,
for they are God's children.
I should welcome the sick to my feast,
for they are God's joy.
Let the poor sit with Jesus at the highest place,
and the sick dance with the angels.

God bless the poor and the sick.
God bless our human race and our food.

Scripture

Come, you that are blessed by my Father,
inherit the kingdom prepared for you
from the foundation of the world;
for I was hungry and you gave me food,
I was thirsty and you gave me something to drink,
I was a stranger and you welcomed me,
I was naked and you gave me clothing,
I was sick and you took care of me,
I was in prison and you visited me ...
Truly I tell you,
just as you did it to the least of these
who are members of my family,
you did it to me.
(Matthew 25:34-36, 40)

Quiet Prayer

Sharing/Intercessions

St Brigid's Blessing

May no fire, no flame burn us.
May no lake, no sea drown us.
May no sword, no spear wound us.
May no king, no chief insult us.
May all the birds sing for us.
May all the cattle low for us.
May all the insects buzz for us.
May the angels of God always protect us.

St Patrick (March 17)

I shall give you as a light to the nations,
that my salvation may reach
to the end of the earth.
(Isaiah 49:6)

Focusing

Scripture

Now the word of the Lord came to me saying,
'Before I formed you in the womb I knew you,
and before you were born I consecrated you;
I appointed you a prophet to the nations.'
Then I said, 'Ah, Lord God!
Truly I do not know how to speak, for I am only a boy.'
But the Lord said to me, 'Do not say, "I am only a boy";
for you shall go to all to whom I send you,
and you shall speak whatever I command you.
Do not be afraid of them,
for I am with you to deliver you, says the Lord.'
(Jeremiah 1:4-8)

The seventy returned with joy, saying,
'Lord, in your name even the demons submit to us!'
He said to them,
'I watched Satan fall from heaven like a flash of lightning.
See, I have given you authority to tread on snakes and scorpions,
and over all the power of the enemy, and nothing will hurt you.
Nevertheless do not rejoice at this, that the spirits submit to you,
but rejoice that your names are written in heaven.'
(Luke 10:17-20)

Then an angel of the Lord stood before them,
and the glory of the Lord shone around them, and they were terrified.
But the angel said to them, 'Do not be afraid; for see –
I am bringing you news of great joy for all the people.'
(Luke 2:9-10)

Quiet Reflection

What is the news of great joy that Patrick brought to the people of Ireland?
What news have we been commissioned to share at this time
and in this place in the history of the world?
How will we share it ?

Shared Reflections/Prayers

Prayer of St Patrick

May the strength of God pilot us,
May the power of God preserve us,
May the wisdom of God instruct us,
May the hand of God protect us,
May the way of God direct us,
May the shield of God defend us,
May the host of God guard us,
against snares of evil
and the temptations of the world.

Lenten Prayer of Awakening

In winter moments
I breathe in deeply
the crisp and startled, frost-bitten air...
while believing and rejoicing
that every intake holds
the loving promise
of Spirit and its care

Focusing

We make the sign of the cross
in the hope that we might know its height and its depth,
its width and its breadth,
and the life to which it invites us.
In the name of the Father and the Son and the Holy Spirit.

Lenten Psalm of Awakening

Come, O Life-giving Creator,
and rattle the door latch
of my slumbering heart.
Awaken me as you breathe upon
a winter-wrapped earth,
gently calling to life virgin Spring.

Awaken in these fortified days
of Lenten prayer and discipline
my youthful dream of holiness.
Call me forth from the prison camp
of my numerous past defeats
and my narrow patterns of being
to make my ordinary life extra-ordinarily alive
through the passion of my love.

Show to me during these Lenten days
how to take the daily things of life
and, by submerging them in the sacred—
to infuse them with a great love
for you, O God, and for others.
Guide me to perform simple acts of love and prayer,
the real works of reform and renewal
of this overture to the spring of the Spirit.

O Father of Jesus, Mother of Christ,
help me not to waste these precious Lenten days
of my soul's spiritual springtime.[51]

Quiet Reflection/Shared Prayer

Concluding Prayer

Creator God, in the folly of the cross
you have broken open for us the crown of life.
Give us love for what you command
and a longing for what you promise,
so that amid this world's changes,
our hearts may be awakened to a world of lasting joy.
In the name of the Father and of the Son and of the Holy Spirit.
Amen.

---

51 Edward Hays, *Prayers for a Planetary Pilgrim*, 136

Care in the Desert

Focusing

Scripture

And the Spirit immediately drove him
out into the wilderness.
He was in the wilderness forty days,
tempted by Satan,
and he was with the wild beasts;
and the angels waited on him.
(Mark 1:12-13)

Reflection

> *Lent is a time to learn to travel light,*
> *to clear the clutter*
> *from our crowded lives and*
> *find a space, a desert.*
>
> *Deserts are bleak; no creature*
> *comforts, only a vast expanse of*
> *stillness, sharpening awareness of*
> *Ourselves and*
> *God.*[52]

Quiet Time

What clutter do I need to release from my life?

Where and how do I feel God's angels
looking after me in my desert?

Sharing/Intercessions

Use for closing – 2/21/01

Closing Prayer

Loving God,
as we make our Lenten journey to new life,
remain with us and guide us in the days ahead.
Help us to recognise and accept your constant care for us
in the deserts of our lives.
We make this our prayer through Christ our Lord. Amen.

---

52 Ann Lewin. Daniel P. Cronin, *Through the Year with Words of Encouragement* (Middlegreen, Slough: St Paul.)

Lent: A Time for Fasting

Focusing

Scripture

Let the same mind be in you as was in Christ Jesus,
who, though he was in the form of God,
did not regard equality with God as something to be exploited,
but emptied himself, taking the form of a slave,
being born in human likeness.
And being found in human form, he humbled himself
and became obedient to the point of death – even death on a cross.
Therefore God also highly exalted him …
(Philippians 2:5-9)

Is not this the fast that I choose:
to loose the bonds of injustice, to undo the thongs of the yoke,
to let the oppressed go free, and to break every yoke?
Is it not to share your bread with the hungry,
and bring the homeless poor into your house;
when you see the naked, to cover them,
and not to hide yourself from your own kin?
… if you offer your food to the hungry
and satisfy the needs of the afflicted,
then your light shall rise in the darkness
and your gloom will be like the noonday.
The Lord will guide you continually,
and satisfy your needs in parched places,
and make your bones strong;
and you shall be like a watered garden,
like a spring of water, whose waters never fail.
(Isaiah 58:6-7, 10-11)

Reflection

More and more I am beginning to realise that when we are called to fast that what we are being invited to is not as much an experience of going without as an experience of going within.

The true fast is a self-emptying; a ridding from the body, mind and heart of all the excess. It is an uncluttering, a freeing of the pathway to our inner self – to that place where we can encounter God at the deepest of levels.

When we have embraced God's presence in our very being we are ready to make the movement from within to without. It is a movement that leads us to act and be in the world as Christ – to be God's presence of love, mercy and compassion to all we encounter, knowing that God will be our guide, our strength, our sustenance.

Quiet Prayer

Shared Reflections/Intercessions

Closing Prayer

God be in us this day,
God ever with us stay
God be in the night
Keep us by thy light
God be in our hearts
God abide, never depart.[53]

---

53 David Adam, *The Edge of Glory,* 19 (adapted)

Lent: A Time for Giving

Focusing

Scripture

He looked up and saw rich people putting their gifts into the treasury; he also saw a poor widow put in two small copper coins. He said, 'Truly I tell you, this poor widow has put in more than all of them; for all of them have contributed out of their abundance, but she out of her poverty has put in all she had to live on.' *(Luke 21:1-4)*

Reflection

Then said a rich man, Speak to us of Giving. And he answered:
You give but little when you give of your possessions.
It is when you give of yourself that you truly give.
For what are your possessions but things you keep and guard
for fear you may need them tomorrow? ...

And what is fear of need but need itself?
Is not dread of thirst when your well is full,
the thirst that is unquenchable?
There are those who give little of the much which they have –
and they give it for recognition
and their hidden desire makes their gifts unwholesome.
And there are those who have little and give it all.
These are the believers in life and the bounty of life,
and their coffer is never empty.
There are those who give with joy, and that joy is their reward.
And there are those who give with pain, and that pain is their baptism.
And there are those who give and know not pain in giving,
nor do they seek joy, nor give with mindfulness of virtue;
They give as in yonder valley the myrtle breathes its fragrance into space.

Through the hands of such as these God speaks,
and from behind their eyes he smiles upon the earth.
It is well to give when asked,
but it is better to give unasked, through understanding;
And to the open-handed the search for one who shall receive
is joy greater than giving.
And is there aught you would withhold?
All you have shall some day be given;
Therefore give now, that the season of giving may be yours
and not your inheritors.[54]

Quiet Time

Shared Reflections/Intercessions

Closing Prayer

Compassionate God,
you bless us with the abundance of your love
and grace us with the gift of your eternal presence.
In this Lenten time give us the wisdom to recognise our poverty
and the compassion to share it's treasure
with our brothers and sisters.
We ask this through your Son Jesus Christ, who gave his life for us.

---

54 Kahlil Gibran, *The Prophet*, London: William Heinemann, distributed by Pan Books, 1980),
24, 27

Lent: A Time for Returning

Return to me with all your heart,
with fasting, with weeping, and with mourning;
rend your hearts and not your clothing.
Return to the Lord, your God,
for he is gracious and merciful,
slow in anger, and abounding in steadfast love.
(Joel 2:12-13)

Focusing

Reflection

I have been meditating on the story of the prodigal son. It is a story about returning. For the son, returning to his father was a necessity for staying alive. He realised that he had sinned, but this realisation came about because sin had brought him close to death. The father didn't require any higher motivation. His love was so total and unconditional that he simply welcomed his son home. This is a very encouraging thought. God does not require a pure heart before embracing us. Even if we return only because following our desires has failed to bring happiness, God will take us back. Even if we return because being a Christian brings us more peace than being a pagan, God will receive us. Even if we return because our sins did not offer as much satisfaction as we had hoped, God will take us back. Even if we return because we could not make it on our own, God will receive us. God's love does not require any explanations about why we are returning, God is glad to see us home and wants to give us all we desire, just for being home. So why delay? God is standing there with open arms, waiting to embrace me. He won't ask any questions about my past. Just having me back is all he desires.[55]

Scripture

Do not fear, for I have redeemed you;
I have called you by name, you are mine.
When you pass through the waters, I will be with you;
and through the rivers, they shall not overwhelm you;
when you walk through fire, you shall not be burned,
and the flame will not consume you ...
Because you are precious in my sight,
and honoured, and I love you.
(Isaiah 43:1-2,4)

Thoughts for Reflection

If God can respond to me in such love and forgiveness,
how can I respond to those whom I encounter?
As a church, how can we be a body
of forgiveness and reconciliation in the world?

Sharing/Intercessions

Closing Prayer

Lord of our heart, give us vision to inspire us.
Lord of our heart, give us wisdom to direct us.
Lord of our heart, give us courage to strengthen us.
Lord of our heart, give us trust to console us.
Lord of our heart, give us love to mission us.
Lord of our heart, give us grace to root our lives in You.[56]

---

55 Henri Nouwen, *The Road to Daybreak*, (London: Darton, Longman and Todd, 1989) 72-73
(edited)
56 Robert Van de Weyer, *Celtic Fire: An Anthology of Celtic Christian Literature* (London: Darton,
Longman and Todd, 1990), 93-94 (adapted)

An Easter Prayer of Rebirth

Why do you look for the living among the dead?
He is not here, but has risen.
(Luke 24:5)

Focusing

Scripture

'And you shall know that I am the Lord,
when I open your graves,
and bring you up from your graves, O my people.
I will put my spirit within you, and you shall live,
and I will place you on your own soil;
then you shall know that I, the Lord,
have spoken and will act,' says the Lord.
(Ezekiel 37:13-14)

And very early on the first day of the week,
when the sun had risen, they went to the tomb.
They had been saying to one another,
'Who will roll away the stone for us from the entrance to the tomb?'
When they looked up, they saw that the stone,
which was very large, had already been rolled back.
As they entered the tomb, they saw a young man,
dressed in a white robe, sitting on the right side;
and they were alarmed.

But he said to them, 'Do not be alarmed;
you are looking for Jesus of Nazareth, who was crucified.
He has been raised; he is not here.
Look, there is the place they laid him.
But go, tell his disciples and Peter
that he is going ahead of you to Galilee;
there you will see him, just as he told you.'
(Mark 16:2-7)

Quiet Time

From what grave is God calling me during this Easter time?
To what life is God inviting me?

Shared Reflection/Prayer

Closing Prayer

God who calls us from the grave,
who has rolled away the stones that have imprisoned us,
give us courageous hearts, inspired by the Holy Spirit,
to emerge from our graves into the joy of the way
– of life – of rebirth – of Christ. Amen.

RCIA — Dialogue
April 25, 2001

Embracing the Gifts of Easter

Easter dawns…
we greet God's holy season,
seeking, sensing resurrection's rays.
They will fill our bones, our hearts, our spirits,
and spur us forward to newer days.

Focusing

An Easter Embrace

I welcome you Easter
and invite your many gifts
to the deep, deep recesses of my soul …

Easter Light bathe me
in the warm, nurturing radiance of your glow;
burn passionately through me,
proclaiming the dazzling wonderment of resurrection.

Easter Word echo again and again
the story of our salvation – yesterday, today and forever;
resound from every human heart, from womb to tomb,
the sacred story which is ours to share.

Easter Water douse, drench, drown me
with your water of life;
cleanse my soul and wash over me
with the torrents of your love
that bring me to birth once more.

Easter Bread break open my body
to receive your nourishment, strengthen me
to share in building your body here on earth;
bring to life the wilderness and the city
with the manna of faith in Christ.

Easter Wine pour forth your love
to the desert and the ocean,
flow freely through us, that all may drink deeply
from the cup of life.

Easter Cross proclaim in your height and your depth,
your width and your breadth,
the transformation of all who embrace you;
from shame to glory, from passion to resurrection,
from agony to ecstasy, stand visible
through your people, as a sign of redemption and hope.

I welcome you Easter,
I sit in your presence and contemplate you awhile
and truly I exult: Christ is risen; Deo Gratias; Thanks be to God.

Quiet Time/Shared Prayer

Concluding Prayer

Creator God,
out of the depth of your love you called us to new life in Christ.
As we rejoice in the resurrection, may our lives and our work together
echo the many gifts you have blessed us with for a purpose.
May all our being resound the glory of your name as we say,
Glory be to the Father and to the Son, and to the Holy Spirit,
as it was in the beginning, is now, and ever shall be,
world without end, Amen. Alleluia!

Prayer of an Easter People

Focusing

Christ yesterday and today
the beginning and the end
Alpha and Omega
all time belongs to him
and all the ages.
To him be glory and power
through every age for ever.
(Easter vigil, Lighting of the Easter Candle)

Scripture

But the angel said to the women,
'Do not be afraid;
I know that you are looking for Jesus who was crucified.
He is not here; for he has been raised, as he said.'
(Matthew 28:5-6)

When he was at the table with them,
he took bread, blessed and broke it, and gave it to them.
Then their eyes were opened, and they recognised him.
(Luke 24:30-31)

If there is any encouragement in Christ,
any consolation from love, any sharing in the Spirit,
any compassion and sympathy,
make my joy complete;
be of the same mind, having the same love,
being in full accord and of one mind.
(Philippians 1:1-2)

Reflection

We are an Easter people! For some reason, at times the memory and pain of Good Friday seems to be an easier reality to grasp. We are more readily able to name and claim suffering. But we are a people called to hope, a people called to believe in and work for transformation, liberation and resurrection.

In partnership with Christ, we can break open God's saving message and share its joy with the world. One in love, one in heart and one in mind, together we can be kingdom builders. And by the fruits of our labour we can declare to those who have eyes to see, to those who have ears to hear, that there is good reason to proclaim – Christ is risen, Alleluia, Alleluia. Yes, we are an Easter people and Alleluia is, indeed, our song.

Quiet Time

Shared Prayer

Concluding Prayer

Christ Jesus, you call us to bring your joy to the world. *Alleluia!*
You invite us to be your Body on earth. *Alleluia!*
You mission us to reach out to the fearful and weak. *Alleluia!*
You empower us to reveal your presence to a weary world. *Alleluia!*
You enthuse us to enter deeper into a life assured of resurrection. *Alleluia!*

Be with us Lord, as we continue our pilgrim journey as an Easter people.
Guide our footsteps with the light of Easter faith,
that we may walk in your ways.
We ask this through Christ our Lord, who has risen from the dead.
Alleluia. Amen.

A Pentecost Prayer

Invitation to Prayer

God be with us – *Amen*
The Lord be with you – *And with your spirit too*
The Father be with us – *Amen*
The Creator be with you – *And with your spirit too*
Jesus be with us – *Amen*
The Saviour be with you – *And with your spirit too*
The Spirit be with us – *Amen*
The strengthener be with you – *And with your spirit too*
The Trinity be with us – *Amen*
The Sacred Three be over you – *And with your spirit too.*
God be with us – *Amen.*57

Quiet Time

A Pentecost Sequence

Come, Spirit who is our Light,
Shine among the shadows within.
Warm and transform our hearts.
    Come, Spirit who makes a home in us.
    Draw us to the treasures of your dwelling.
    Reveal to us the inner journey of love.
Come, Spirit, Comforter and Consoler.
Heal the wounded. Soothe the anxious.
Be consolation for all who grieve and ache.
    Come, Spirit who energises our being.
    Keep us from the tangles of toil and travail.
    Lead us to moments of prayer and play.
Come, Spirit, consuming Fire of Love,
Fill us with enthusiasm for your vision.
May the desire for truth be vibrant in us.

Come, Spirit, joy of our souls.
Dance amid life's hills and valleys.
Encircle us with the delights of your dance.
Come, Spirit of wisdom and insight.
Draw us towards your goodness and light.
Direct our growth and guide our ways.
    Come, Spirit, strength of wounded ones.
    Be warmth in hearts of those grown cold.
    Empower the powerless, rekindle the weary.
Come Spirit, source of our peace.
Deepen in us the action of peacemakers.
Heal the divisions that ravage the earth.[58]

Reflections/Intercessions

Closing Prayer

Come, Holy Spirit,
breathe new life into your people.
Show us the true meaning of the gospel
and enkindle our hearts
with a love that will transform our lives.
Grant us the unity for which Jesus prayed
now and forever. Amen.

---

57 David Adam, *The Edge of Glory*, 63
58 Joyce Rupp, *May I Have this Dance?* 69-70

The Energy of the Spirit

Focusing

Scripture

Likewise the Spirit helps us in our weakness; for we do not know how to pray as we ought, but that very Spirit intercedes with sighs too deep for words. And God, who searches the heart, knows what is the mind of the Spirit, because the Spirit intercedes for the saints according to the will of God. *(Romans 8:26-27)*

Intercessions

When we come face to face with the challenge of self-giving; when we are asked to go the extra mile, to take the risk of reaching out to another, to offer forgiveness to the heart that rejects us ...
   Response: Spirit of God, fill us with the energy of your love.

When our world seems bleak; when we walk with sadness written on our soul; when we have days when everything goes wrong ...
   Response: Spirit of God, stir the energy of your joy within us.

When someone needs a simple gesture of thoughtfulness; when a look of love is all that another asks of us; when a good word could take the sting out of the gossip of foes ...
   Response: Spirit of God, create in us the energy of your kindness.

As we face the shadow of our inner world, or peer into the darkness of our outer world; as we struggle to believe in our own gifts and blessings ...
   Response: Spirit of God, strengthen in us the energy of your goodness.

In those difficult times when fear threatens to drown our trust in you; during those trying experiences when we are tempted to doubt all the ways we have known you ...
   Response: Spirit of God, renew in us the energy of trusting in you.

When anxiety and concern take over our spirit; when restlessness or bordeom holds sway over us; when our world cries out in distress and turmoil ...
   Response: Spirit of God, deepen in us the energy of your peace.

On those days when we hurry too much; at those times when anger flares because our agendas aren't met; when we stop giving people understanding and acceptance ...
   Response: Spirit of God, draw us towards the energy of your patience

As we walk on the edges of life and death; as we struggle with the disciplines of spiritual growth; as we yearn to be faithful amidst the many changes of inner and outer growth ...
   Response: Spirit of God, move us with the energy of your guidance.[59]

Quiet Prayer

Concluding Prayer
Spirit of God, breathed into our hearts in Jesus' resurrection
lift us up with new life, new courage, new passion today.
Spirit of God, breathed into our midst in Jesus' resurrection
transform us with new fellowship, new vision, new joy today.
Spirit of God, breathed into the world in Jesus' resurrection
work through us to change the face of the earth.

---

59 Joyce Rupp, *May I Have this Dance?* 76-78 (adapted)

Searching for the Spirit

Come, Holy Spirit, fill the hearts of the faithful
and kindle in us the fire of your love. Alleluia.

Focusing

Scripture

On the morning of the third day there was thunder and lightning flashes, as well as a thick cloud on the mountain, and a blast of a trumpet so loud that all the people who were in the camp trembled. Moses brought the people out of the camp to meet God. They took their stand at the foot of the mountain. Now Mount Sinai was wrapped in smoke, because the Lord had descended on it in fire; the smoke went up like the smoke of a kiln, while the whole mountain shook violently. As the blast of the trumpet grew louder and louder, Moses would speak and God would answer him in thunder. When the Lord descended upon Mount Sinai, on the top of the mountain, the Lord summoned Moses to the top of the mountain, and Moses went up. *(Exodus 19:16-20)*

Elijah got up, and ate and drank; then he went in the strength of that food forty days and forty nights to Horeb the mount of God. At that place he came to a cave, and spent the night there. Then the word of the Lord came to him, saying ... 'Go out and stand on the mountain before the Lord, for the Lord is about to pass by.' Now there was a great wind, so strong that it was splitting mountains and breaking rocks to pieces before the Lord, but the Lord was not in the wind; and after the wind an earthquake, but the Lord was not in the earthquake; and after the earthquake a fire, but the Lord was not in the fire; and after the fire, a sound of sheer silence. When Elijah heard it, he wrapped his face in his mantle and went out and stood at the entrance of the cave ...
(1 Kings 19:8-9, 11-13)

Reflection

The Spirit, elusive and 'blowing where it will', is not as unknown to us as we sometimes think. That we cannot confine and define its nature does not mean we do not know it. Curiously, we know and recognise the Spirit manifest in the light and liveliness, the creativity or energy, the wisdom or the reverence in the life of the other. For it is through others that the Spirit ministers to us. And it is we who can draw out the Spirit in the other. We know it less well in ourselves and squirm self-consciously when others mention our own creative Spirit. But the Spirit dwells in our hearts so that it can minister beyond itself, so it can 'matter' in the life of another.[60]

Quiet Time

Intercessions

Litany

Spirit of light, let the fire of your wisdom burn brightly within us.
Spirit of silence, in the still moment may we be open to God's presence.
Spirit of courage, dispel the fear that lingers in our hearts.
Spirit of fire, engulf us with the passion of Christ's love.
Spirit of peace, help us to be attentive to God's word in the world.
Spirit of joy, enthuse us to proclaim aloud the Good News.
Spirit of love, compel us to open ourselves to the needs of others.
Spirit of power, bestow the gift of your strength upon us.
Spirit of truth, guide us to walk in the way of Christ.

---

60 Gertrud Mueller Nelson, *To Dance with God* (New York: Paulist Press, 1986) 90

Trinity

Focusing

We are enclosed in the Father
and we are enclosed in the Son
and we are enclosed in the Holy Spirit.
And the Father is enclosed in us
and the Son is enclosed in us
and the Holy Spirit is enclosed in us;
Almightiness, All Wisdom, All Goodness;
One God, one Lord.
(Julian of Norwich)

Scripture

When the fulness of time had come, God sent his Son ... so that we might receive adoption as children. And because you are children, God has sent the Spirit of his Son into our hearts, crying 'Abba! Father!' So you are no longer a slave but a child, and if a child then also an heir. *(Galatians 4:4-7)*

Reflection

If God as primordial origin is pictured as the sun,
and God incarnate as the beam of that same light streaming to the earth
(Christ the sunbeam),
then Spirit is the point of light that actually arrives
and affects the earth with warmth and energy.
And it is all the one shining light.

Again, triune holy mystery may be pictured
as an upwelling spring of water,
the river that flows outward from this source,
and the irrigation channel where the water meets and moistens the earth
– again, Spirit. And it is all the one flowing water.

Yet again, the triune God can be compared to a flowering plant
with its deep, invisible root,
its green stem reaching into the world from that root,
and its flower (Spirit) which opens to spread beauty and fragrance
and to fructify the earth with fruit and seed.
And it is all the one living plant.

The point for our pondering is that calling the mystery of God Spirit
signifies the active presence of God in this ambiguous world.
Whether the Spirit be pictured as the warmth and light given by the sun,
the life-giving water from the spring,
or the flower filled with seeds from the root,
what we are actually signifying is God drawing near and passing by
in vivifying, sustaining, renewing and liberating power
in the midst of historical struggle.[61]

Quiet Prayer/Shared Prayer

Concluding Prayer

To you,
Eternal Source of all Being,
Word of Life,
Holy Spirit,
be glory for ever and ever. Amen

---

61 Elizabeth Johnson, *She Who Is; The Mystery of God in Feminist Theological Discourse* (New York: Crossroad, 1993), 127. The images are drawn from Tertullian.

St Columba (June 9)

The storm may roar within me,
My heart may low be laid,
But God is round about me,
And can I be dismayed?

Focusing

St Columba's Psalm

Delightful I think it to be in the bosom of an isle, on the peak of a rock,
that I might often see there the calm of the sea.

That I might see its heavy waves over the glittering ocean,
as they chant a melody to their Father on their eternal course.

That I might see its smooth strand of clear headlands, no gloomy thing;
that I might hear the voice of the wondrous birds, a joyful tune.

That I might hear the sound of the shallow waves against the rocks;
that I might hear the cry by the graveyard, the noise of the sea.

That I might see its spendid flocks of birds over the full-watered ocean;
that I might see its mighty whales, greatest of wonders.

That I might see its ebb and its flood-tide in their flow;
that this might be my name, a secret I tell,
'He who turned his back on Ireland.'

That contrition of heart should come upon me as I watch it;
that I might bewail my many sins, difficult to declare.

That I might bless the Lord who has power over all,
Heaven with its pure host of angels, earth, ebb, flood-tide.

That I might pore on one of my books, good for my soul;
a while kneeling for beloved Heaven, a while at psalms.

A while gathering dulse from the rocks, a while fishing;
a while giving food to the poor, a while in my cell.

A while meditating upon the Kingdom of Heaven, holy is the redemption;
a while at labour not too heavy; it would be delightful![62]

Quiet Prayer

Shared Prayer/Reflections

Concluding Prayer
May the God of Jesus Christ
who inspired Columba
with love of nature and passion for the gospel
inspire our hearts.
May we enjoy God's world;
may we rejoice in God's gospel;
may we find joy in God's people.
Through Christ our Lord. Amen.

---

62 Kenneth Hurlstone Jackson, *A Celtic Miscellany: Translations from the Celtic Literature*
(London: Penguin, 1975), 279-80

In the mind-steps, heart-steps, foot-steps of Peter

Focusing

First-Steps

But when Simon Peter saw it, he fell down at Jesus' knees, saying, 'Go away from me, Lord, for I am a sinful man!' ... Jesus said to Simon, 'Do not be afraid; from now on you will be catching people.' *(Luke 5:8, 10)*

Like Peter, Lord, I am inadequate. May I not allow my smallness obscure your attractiveness. Now more than ever may I believe in myself as a catcher of people, that through me other people can experience your new life.

Heart-steps

So Peter got out of the boat, started walking on the water, and came toward Jesus. But when he noticed the strong wind, he became frightened, and beginning to sink, he cried out, 'Lord, save me!' Jesus immediately reached out his hand and caught him, saying to him, 'You of little faith, why did you doubt?' *(Matthew 14:29-31)*

Lord, my heart too feels a mix of courage and fear, determination and doubt. In these troubled times for your church, may I not stick cautiously to the safe footholds I am familiar with. Give me courage to walk on the water to you. Grant me a heart willing to risk because it trusts in you.

Mind-steps

Then Peter came and said to him, 'Lord, if another member of the church sins against me, how often should I forgive? As many as seven times?' Jesus said to him, 'Not seven times, but, I tell you, seventy-seven times.' *(Matthew 18:21-22)*

Your way, O Lord, demands from me a new way of seeing, just as it did of Peter. Breathe your Spirit of wisdom upon me, that I may understand and accept the far-reaching implications of following you. Never allow me to reduce my discipleship to manageable proportions.

Foot-steps

Peter said to him, 'Though all become deserters because of you, I will never desert you' ... He took with him Peter and the two sons of Zebedee ... Then he came to the disciples and found them sleeping ... Peter was following him at a distance, as far as the courtyard of the high priest ... A servant girl came to him and said, 'You also were with Jesus the Galilean.' But he denied it ... *(Matthew 26:33, 37, 40, 58, 69-70)*

Like Peter, Lord, my footsteps falter. I follow close behind you, then my legs give way to tiredness; I keep a distance between us and then I turn away from you. I pray for a realistic sense of where I am weak and where I am strong, and of what I am able for. Grant me the humility to find my strength in you.

Full-steps

And he said to him, 'Lord, you know everything; you know that I love you.' Jesus said to him, 'Feed my sheep. Very truly, I tell you, when you were younger, you used to fasten your own belt and to go wherever you wished. But when you grow old, you will stretch out your hands, and someone else will fasten a belt around you and take you where you do not wish to go' ... After this he said to him, 'Follow me.' *(John 21:17-19)*

Lord, with both joy and shame, I gather up the moments of courage and conviction, of confusion and consternation, of commitment and cowardice, that have made up my life as your beloved disciple. Call me now a second time, as you did Peter, and allow me to begin again. Put a young vision into my old soul, that I may love you more than ever.

Used 10/4/00 @ staff

Francis of Assissi (October 4)

Focusing

Scripture

Do not worry about your life, what you will eat, or about your body, what you will wear. For life is more than food, and the body more than clothing. Consider the ravens; they neither sow nor reap, they have neither storehouse nor barn, and yet God feeds them. Of how much more value are you than the birds! And can any of you by worrying add a single hour to your span of life? If then you are not able to do so small a thing as that, why do you worry about the rest? ... Instead, strive for his kingdom, and these things will be given to you as well.
(Luke 12:22-26, 31)

The Canticle of Brother Son

Most high, all powerful, all good, Lord!
All praise is yours, all glory, all honour and all blessing.
To you alone, Most High, do they belong.
No mortal lips are worthy to pronounce your name.
All praise be yours, my Lord, with all that you have made,
and first, my Lord, brother Sun, who brings the day,
and light you give to us through him.
How beautiful is he, how radiant in all his splendour!
Of you, Most High, he bears the likeness.
All praise be yours, my Lord, through sister Moon and Stars;
in the heavens you have made them, bright and precious and fair.
All praise be yours, my Lord, through brothers Wind and Air,
and fair and stormy, all the weather's moods
by which you cherish all that you have made.

All praise be yours, my Lord, through sister Water,
so useful, so lowly, precious and pure.
All praise be yours, my Lord, through brother Fire,
through whom you brighten up the night.
How beautiful is he, full of power and strength!
All praise be yours, my Lord, through sister Earth, our mother,
who feeds us in her sovereignty
and produces various fruits with coloured flowers and herbs.
All praise be yours, my Lord,
though those who grant pardon for love of you;
through those who endure sickness and trial;
happy those who endure in peace;
by you, Most High, they will be crowned.
All praise be yours, my Lord, through sister Death,
from whose embrace no mortal can escape.
Woe to those who die in mortal sin;
happy those she finds doing your will.
The second death can do no harm to them.
Praise and bless my Lord,
and give him thanks and serve him with great humility.

Quiet Prayer/Shared Prayer

Conclusion

Make me a channel of your peace;
where there is hatred let me bring your love;
where there is injury, your pardon Lord,
and where there's doubt, true faith in you.
    O Master grant that I may never seek
    so much to be consoled as to console;
    to be understood as to understand;
    to be loved as to love with all my soul.
Make me a channel of your peace;
it is in pardoning that we are pardoned;
in giving to each one that we receive
and in dying that we're born to eternal life.

Autumn's Peaceful Ebbing

Focusing

Autumn Psalm of Fearlessness

I am surrounded by a peaceful ebbing
    as creation bows to the mystery of life;
    all that grows and lives must give up life,
    yet it does not really die.
As plants surrender their life,
    bending, brown and wrinkled,
    and yellow leaves of trees
    float to my lawn like parachute troops,
    they do so in a sea of serenity.

I hear no fearful cries from creation,
    no screams of terror,
    as death daily devours
    once-green and growing life.
Peaceful and calm is autumn's swan song,
    for she understands
    that hidden in winter's death-grip
    is spring's openhanded
    full-brimmed breath of life.

It is not a death rattle that sounds
    over fields and backyard fences;
    rather I hear a lullaby
    softly swaying upon the autumn wind.
Sleep in peace, all that lives;
    slumber secure, all that is dying,
    for in every fall there is the rise
    whose sister's name is spring.[63]

Scripture

If we have died with him, we will also live with him;
if we endure, we will also reign with him. *(2 Timothy 2:11-12)*

And this is the will of him who sent me,
that I should lose nothing of all that he has given me,
but should raise it up on the last day. *(John 6:39)*

Quiet Time

Shared Prayer

Concluding Prayer

We praise you, Lord, for what Autumn teaches.
We praise you for the beauty and colour and drama
you have put into what is dying.
Teach us to die to ourselves, to give our all,
with such grace and energy and spirit,
that your name will be glorified and held high.
Glory be, as Autumn teaches,
to the Father and the Son and the Holy Spirit,
now and forever. Amen

---

63 Edward Hays, *Prayers for a Planetary Pilgrim*, 120

November: In Communion with the Dead

Focusing

> *God calls each one by name. Everyone's name is sacred ...*
> *It demands respect as a sign of the dignity of the one who bears it.*
> *(Catechism, 2158)*

Scripture

Do not fear, for I have redeemed you. I have called you by name, you are mine. *(Isaiah 43:1)*

Can a mother forget her nursing child, or show no compassion for the child of her womb? Even these may forget, yet I will never forget you. See, I have inscribed you on the palms of my hands. *(Isaiah 49:15-16)*

I will give them an everlasting name that shall not be cut off. *(Isaiah 56:5)*

You shall be called by a new name that the mouth of the Lord will give. You shall be a crown of beauty in the hand of the Lord ... You shall no more be termed 'Forsaken ... but you shall be called 'My delight Is in Her'. *(Isaiah 62:2-4)*

Rejoice that your names are written in heaven. *(Luke 10:20)*

Quiet Time

Bring to mind the names of those you have known who have died...
so many names...
unlock your memory and acknowledge them all as they pass before you...

Shared Prayer

Intercessions

We thank you Lord for those dead who were so dear to us,
from whom such goodness flowed.
We pray that all they held sacred
and everything in which they were wonderful
will continue to mean much to us
and go on living in our hearts and lives. *Lord hear us.*

Let us reach out and pray for all who mourn the death
of a child or a parent, a brother or sister, a friend or relative.
Let us pray for all who have suffered an unspeakable loss,
and for those who go on blindly, unable to overcome their sorrow.
Let us pray for all who are discouraged
that they may not hate the light of life
but that they may keep an open heart.. *Lord hear us.*

Let us pray for all who die and are not mourned
but are ignored in death like a stone by the roadside.
Let us pray for all who are lost in war and prison,
for those who have committed suicide
and for those who are lonely in life or death,
that God may hear them, and keep them in his heart.. *Lord hear us.*[64]

In all our prayers we give thanks to Jesus Christ our brother
who died our death so that we might live his life.

---

64 Huub Oosterhuis, *Your Word is Near,* 86-89 (adapted)

Deanery: 12/8/99

cMary Light of Disciples

*We are all meant to be mothers of God
because God is always needing to be born.
(Meister Eckhart)*

Focusing

Reflection

I beg you to listen to what the Lord had to say when he stretched out his hand towards his disciples; 'Here are my mother and my brothers and sisters'; and 'Whoever does the will of my Father in heaven is my brother and my sister and my mother'. Are we to take it from this that the Virgin Mary did not do the will of the Father? ... Indeed and indeed she did the Father's will and it is a greater thing for her that she was Christ's disciple than that she was his mother. It is a happier thing to be his disciple than to be his mother ...

See if it isn't as I say. The Lord was journeying on and the crowds were following him. He did a work of divine power and this woman in the crowd cried out; 'Blessed is the womb that bore you and the breasts that you sucked.' But they must not think that blessedness lay in bodily relationship, so what did the Lord answer? 'Blessed rather are those who hear the word of God and keep it.' Therefore Mary is blessed because she 'heard the word of God and kept it'. Her mind was filled more fully with Truth than her womb by his flesh ...

Mary is part of the church. She is a holy member of the church; she is the holy member; she is the member above all members; but she is still one member of the whole body... Listen very closely: you are members of Christ's body and you are the body of Christ. And this is how you are what he said: 'Here are my mother and my brothers and my sisters'.
(Augustine, Sermon 25)

Quiet Time

Intercessions

Though perplexed at her calling, Mary responds; 'Here I am, the servant of the Lord, let it be with me according to your word.'
Response: May our lives sing Yes to God with Mary.

In response to the revelation of the shepherds, 'Mary treasured all these words and pondered them in her heart' – it was to be the pattern of her life.
Response: Teach us, Lord, Mary's gift of contemplation.

At the prophecy of Simeon – 'and a sword will pierce your own soul too' – Mary braces herself, in faith and courage, to bear the pain that lies ahead.
Response: May the Spirit of courage sustain our faith as it did Mary's.

In response to the experience of losing her son and then finding him in the temple, Mary 'treasured all these things in her heart.'
Response: May we, like Mary, learn to see more deeply into things.

At the foot of the cross, Mary hears the dying words of her son; 'Woman, here is your son... here is your mother.'
Response: Lord, give us what you gave Mary, a hint of hope when things are dark.

Among the disciples, in the upper room, after the resurrection, Mary is part of the community of prayer.
Response: In company with Mary, may prayer be the heart of our discipleship.

Hail Holy Queen ...

Sing your Magnificat

Rejoice in the Lord always; again I will say, Rejoice.
(Philippians 4:4)

Focusing

Scripture

My soul glorifies you, O Lord,
my spirit rejoices in you my Saviour,
for you have looked with favour on your lowly servant.
Surely, from this day forth, all generations will call me blessed.
You, the Mighty One, have done great things for me,
holy is your name.
Your mercy is for those who fear you, from generation to generation.
You have shown the strength of your arm;
you have scattered the proud-hearted.
You have brought down the powerful from their thrones,
and have lifted up the lowly.
You have filled the hungry with good things,
while sending the rich away empty.
You have helped your servant Israel, in remembrance of your mercy,
according to the promise you made to our ancestors,
to Abraham and to his descendants forever.
(Based on Luke 1:47-55)

Quiet Time

We each have our own Magnificat to sing.
Where is there Magnificat in my life? my world?
What is my poverty and rejoicing?
How do I sing with Mary?

Shared Prayer/Reflections

Concluding Prayer

Blessed be the God of Israel,
hearing the cries of God's sons and daughters.
Response: God has done great things for us; holy is the name of God.

Blessed be the God of Israel,
glorified in the great Yes of Mary.
Response: God has done great things for us; holy is the name of God.

Blessed be the God of Israel,
born again in the heart of each disciple.
Response: God has done great things for us; holy is the name of God.

Blessed be the God of Israel,
raining Righteousness upon the earth.
Response: God has done great things for us; holy is the name of God.

Glory be to the Father and to the Son and to the Holy Spirit;
as it was in the beginning, is now and ever shall be,
world without end. Amen.

Mary – Through the Windows of the Gospels

Mary is above all the example of that worship
that consists in making one's life an offering to God.
(Paul VI, Marialis Cultis, 21)

Focusing

Scripture

But she was much perplexed by his words and pondered what sort of greeting this might be. *(Luke 1:29)*

Here am I, the servant of the Lord; let it be with me according to your word. *(Luke 1:38)*

My soul magnifies the Lord and my spirit rejoices in God my saviour. *(Luke 1:47)*

But Mary treasured all these words and pondered them in her heart. *(Luke 2:19)*

And the child's father and mother were amazed at what was being said about him. Then Simeon blessed them and said to his mother Mary, 'This child is destined for the falling and the risomg of many in Israel, and to be a sign that will be opposed, so that the inner thoughts of many may be revealed – and a sword will pierce your own soul too.' *(Luke 2:33-35)*

When his parents saw him they were astonished, and his mother said to him, 'Child, why have you treated us like this?' *(Luke 2:48)*

Then his mother and his brothers came to him, but they could not reach him because of the crowd. And he was told, 'Your mother and your brothers are standing outside, wanting to see you.' But he said to them, 'My mother and my brothers are those who hear the word of God and do it.' *(Luke 8:19-21)*

His mother said to the servants, 'Do whatever he tells you.' *(John 2:5)*

When Jesus saw his mother and the disciple whom he loved standing beside her, he said to his mother, 'Woman, here is your Son.' Then he said to the disciple, 'Here is your mother.' And from that hour the disciple took her into his home. *(John 19:26-27)*

Quiet Reflection

Choose one of the above quotes
and spend some time reflecting upon it
in the light of your own life experience .

Shared Reflections/Prayers

Closing Prayer

Gentle Mary, we pray …
for hearts of courage that we may accept the will of God.

Attentive Mary, we pray …
for hearts of wisdom that we may hear the word of God
and respond to it in our lives.

Compassionate Mary, we pray …
for hearts of love that we may act in a spirit of charity and service.

Mother Mary, we pray …
for hearts of discipleship that we may be led to live in God's ways.

Hail Mary…

Index of Themes

Index of Names

Index of Scripture Passages